A PLAYWORKER'S GUIDE
TO UNDERSTANDING
CHILDREN'S BEHAVIOUR

A PLAYWORKER'S GUIDE TO UNDERSTANDING CHILDREN'S BEHAVIOUR

Working with the 8–12 Age Group

Andrea Clifford-Poston

Foreword by
Liz Roberts

(Editor of *Nursery World*)

KARNAC

First published in 2008 by
Karnac Books Ltd
118 Finchley Road, London NW3 5HT

British Library Cataloguing in Publication Data

A C.I.P. for this book is available from the British Library

ISBN: 978–1–85575–494–2

Designed, typeset and produced by
Florence Production Ltd, Stoodleigh, Devon
www.florenceproduction.co.uk

Printed in Great Britain by Biddles Ltd., Kings Lynn, Norfolk
www.karnacbooks.com

Disclaimer

Wherever actual quotations and family stories have been used permission has been sought and kindly granted. However, names, dates and other factors affording recognition of individuals has been changed to protect confidentiality. Any similarity to any child, parent or professional, alive or dead, is therefore purely coincidental.

Some of the views in this book may have occurred earlier in a slightly different form in both *Tweens* and *When Harry Hit Sally*.

Dedication

In memory of Kay Alderdice
who taught me about teaching

and

Anne Wiltsher
who taught me about journalism

About the author:
Andrea Clifford-Poston, M.Ed. is a UKCP registered Educational Psychotherapist and has over thirty years experience of working with children, parents and professionals in schools, clinics, hospitals and the home. Andrea trained initially as a primary school teacher and taught in various London schools. For sixteen years she was the Teacher in Charge at the Child Development Centre, Charing Cross Hospital, and for many years a Visiting Lecturer to the Music Therapy Training Course at Roehampton University. Andrea has contributed articles to a number of leading childcare magazines including *Nursery World* and *The Times Parent Forum*. She has also written papers for teachers and professionals.

For the past thirteen years she has been in private practice as a Child and Family Mental Health Specialist. She acts as a consultant to and runs training courses for professionals working with children.

Andrea is a member of the Guildford Centre for Psychotherapy.

By the same author:
Tweens: What to Expect from, and How to Survive, Your Child's Pre-Teenage Years
(Oneworld, 2005)

When Harry Hit Sally: Understanding Your Child's Behaviour
(Simon & Schuster, 2007)

Contents

Acknowledgements

It was my friend and colleague, Jennie Marlow, who first suggested I write for *Nursery World*. I am grateful to her for opening this new and interesting world to me and for her ongoing interest and support.

Liz Roberts, Editor of *Nursery World*, who has kindly agreed to write the Foreword, has been a constant support and inspiration; Annette Rawstrone and the late Anne Wiltsher, Editors of the "Out of School" supplement have been endlessly patient and encouraging in teaching me to transfer my skills to journalism.

Over the years, numerous colleagues in a variety of professions have read the papers and offered me helpful comments and insights. I am grateful to them all and especially to the out-of-school club workers who have taken time to discuss the papers with me.

I am again particularly grateful to Adam Phillips. He read every paper as it was written and has provided me with an invaluable space in which to develop and find words for my own ideas at the same time as always being able to add a creative and original slant of his own.

My typist, Penny Carter, has again proved that the impossible can be achieved and achieved professionally, on time and with a minimum of fuss!

Many thanks to my agent, Stephanie Ebdon (Paterson Marsh) for her support and encouragement and for doing all the messy bits!

The late Murray Cox FRCP first taught me to think psychodynamically about inappropriate behaviour and modelled an understanding and inclusive approach.

Acknowledgements

Finally, and above all, I thank my husband who has not only proved that man can live by "club sandwich" alone but has also provided the facilitating environment this book needed in order to mature.

Foreword

From humble beginnings, out-of-school clubs have become a major part of the Government's National Childcare Strategy, with £1.1 billion extra funding promised for the extended schools programme over the next few years.

The Government wants every school to provide "extended services", and out-of-school clubs are a central part of that offer. They can make it possible for parents to find their way back into the workforce, and they can help to improve outcomes for children—although those two aims can sometimes seem to be in conflict in both policy and practice!

The big money pot, however, does not translate into riches for individual clubs struggling to survive—they must balance the fees that parents can find hard to afford with their club's outgoings on salaries and resources. And there is a continual stream of new policies, new requirements and additional bureaucracy to deal with.

Yet many dedicated clubs and playworkers continue to shine with enthusiasm and determination to do their best for the children in their care. They have few sources of information, advice and support to help them in their role, but continue day in, day out, to make a difference to families' lives.

This is why Andrea Clifford-Poston's book, *A Play-worker's Guide to Understanding Children's Behaviour*, is much needed. It has at its heart the special and unique relationship between playworkers and the children they care for. It is a relationship that is playful, but one that also needs the adult to be close enough to children to understand the complexities of their family and school life and the effects that may have on their behaviour. They must know how to support children in a sensitive and appropriate way.

So amid all the talk of expansion of services, regulations, outcomes and targets, we must strive to keep the child at the centre. Andrea's book will be essential reading for all playworkers.

Liz Roberts
Editor, *Nursery World*

INTRODUCTION

This book was originally written as a series of monthly articles for the Out-of-School section of *Nursery World*. I was asked to provide articles which would give out-of-school practitioners some guidelines for managing challenging children and behaviour in club. I found the task absorbing.

I began my professional career as a primary school teacher in London in the late 1960s/early 70s. At that time after school club was generally a rather haphazard event. It was often run by a teaching assistant for children in the Early Years department of the school. These children would finish school earlier than their older siblings, and after school club was a room where they were supervised until they could be escorted home.

The quality of these clubs varied enormously: some supervised children while they drew or read or played board games, while others would make club more of an event with a snack and a story.

I have watched out-of-school clubs grow and develop with interest. Now they provide a whole range of functions and activities; they are no longer simply a babysitting service! Out of School Clubs are regularly inspected to ensure they maintain Ofsted standards. Staff have also grown and developed with training and continuous assessments an essential part of the work.

The raising of professional standards has provoked the question "What are Out-of-School Clubs?" Tom Gill, writing in *Nursery World* in 2006, so accurately highlights how the very name "out-of-school club" tells us only what a club is not: it is not school (see Gill, 2006). The name tells us nothing about what club is; he suggests that the Scandinavian name "free club time" gives much more indication of the nature of out-of-school clubs. They are a place where children are free to explore use of the time, space and adults provided as they wish.

Club is a transitional space for children. It is not home and it is not school. It is a third world for children to explore. The role of club is not nearly as clearly defined as that of school. I develop this idea further in the chapter "Acting the Part".

Writing these articles gave me an opportunity to think more about my interest in the overlap in ways of thinking about and managing children in different settings. I have worked as a teacher, an Educational Psychotherapist and a child and family therapist in all the major child settings: school, home, clinics and hospitals. As a young teacher I was involved in voluntary and youth work. I have run regular support groups and training days for professionals working with children, including out-of-school club workers.

In all settings, two factors seem to be crucial to child containment. The first is to understand children's behaviour as a language, as being a way of communicating with adults. The second is that the practitioner's response to the child should be in tune with the professional setting. For example, disruptive behaviour in the classroom should be managed with an educational response. Psychodynamic or behavioural modification theories may inform and colour teachers' responses but that is different from a teacher trying to act as a child's therapist.

But an out-of-school club practitioner does not have such a clearly defined role as a teacher or other professionals. They are interesting people for children; they are not parents and they are not authority figures in the same way as teachers—they *are* authority figures, but because they are working in an informal setting they have the potential to be much more parental with children than other professionals.

Playworkers have much more opportunity for informal and casual conversations and contacts with children. They are also free from target attainments or definite goals. This enables them to explore and develop the group as a means of helping an individual child.

It is also interesting that playworkers are in the position of having a duty of care towards children, like teachers and other professionals, but, unlike teachers, the children are not a captive audience! Most children are able to choose whether or not they attend an out-of-school club. This is very important because out-of-school club is the only organised, non-task orientated organisation that children can choose to attend. There will be some for whom there is no other childcare solution after school or during the holidays but the fact remains that out-of-school club is a voluntary activity.

I hope this book will give playworkers some workable understanding of worrying behaviour in club. It is interesting that whenever I am asked to give a seminar on a topic such as "managing disruptive behaviour", we can guarantee the seminar will be oversubscribed. On one hand this is not surprising as a disruptive child can ruin a club session for everyone including themselves, but it also implies that adults have a fantasy that there is an "expert" or magic answer to troubled and troubling children. And, of course, this is not true. The answer to disruptive behaviour lies in the relationship between that child and the adults around them.

I have highlighted elsewhere (Clifford-Poston, 2007) that the problem with behaviour management techniques with children is that the children have not read the books! Such techniques place the child and the adult at right angles to each other in an almost confrontational style. Sometimes they can be very successful but we all know that what works for one child does not necessarily work for another.

Another risk of using the phrase "behaviour management" is that it also, consciously or unconsciously, sets up a negative connotation in the adult's mind about the child concerned. It is a phrase used exclusively about behaviour considered inappropriate or "bad". No one asks for techniques to manage children's good behaviour—we know how to do that instinctively.

What I hope this book will do is to help club workers to realise that with a bit of thought and understanding it is possible to be just as instinctive in responding to difficult behaviour, and that people will find the phrase "behaviour containment" more positive and empowering than "behaviour management." What I also hope is that this book will highlight what playworkers have to tell teachers and parents about understanding and containing children. The aim is to provide playworkers with a useful resource to enhance their skills as a whole. I also want to provide a book that play leaders can dip into when a particular behavioural issue with a child arises and they feel they have run the gamut of their existing skills.

Each chapter stands alone as an entirety, though you will find some cross-referencing. Equally, I hope reading the whole collection will stimulate playworkers' thinking about their work with children and also extend their repertoire of skills.

Occasionally you may find key thoughts repeated in the material. As I reviewed the chapters it became clear that there were four predominant themes running through them all, and these are the main themes that I will be exploring and developing throughout the book:

- Children use behaviour as a language to communicate with adults.
- Problem behaviour is a problem to the adults; to the child it is a solution to a worry.
- When children cannot put their feelings into words they will make the adult feel what they are feeling.
- How do we know which children to worry about?

Behaviour as a language

By adult standards children have very limited ways of letting adults know they have a problem. When they don't have the words to express themselves, or don't know why they feel worried or unhappy, they are likely to use behaviour to communicate with adults. In this sense, all behaviour has meaning. Sometimes it is easy for adults to understand, for example if a child is crying and upset, we can see they are miserable. Other behaviour is more complex—stealing, for example. The child who steals is not telling you what he wants, he is telling you how he feels about himself inside.

So often adults respond to the child's actual behaviour and not to what the behaviour is trying to communicate. This is not surprising, as children often choose behaviour that does not accurately illustrate their worry. One of the skills of working successfully with children is learning to understand their behaviour as a language. Paediatrician and child analyst Donald Winnicott, writing in the 1950s and 60s, used the phrase "the function of the symptom". By this he meant that we need to try to understand what a child might think they are gaining by behaving in a particular way.

Disruption as a solution

For adults disruptive behaviour is often a problem that they want to eliminate. To the child, disruptive behaviour is a solution—a way of communicating with adults. Whenever you are faced with worrying behaviour from a child, it is always worth asking yourself, "What might this behaviour be a solution to for the child?". When adults understand why a child is behaving the way they are, they are free to come up with their own ways of controlling the behaviour in a manner in which the child feels heard and understood—and consequently under less pressure to repeat inappropriate or undesirable actions.

The key to understanding the child's solution is to think about the exact opposite of the behaviour. We can think of a seven year old, hurt and angry by the arrival of a new baby in the family, who suddenly kicks his playworker in the stomach. At first glance, such aggressive behaviour could be construed as the child not liking the playworker or being angry with the playworker. But this behaviour is much more likely to be his way of showing his longing for adult affection in a dramatic, attention seeking way that makes adults angry. He is then likely to be punished, which leaves him feeling even more anxious and so likely to do even more attention seeking actions, and so a vicious circle develops.

Throughout this book I will develop the theme of how adults often use the phrase "just attention seeking", as though there is something wrong with having needs and needing attention to those needs. No child is "just attention seeking". Such a child as this seven year old is trying to get close to adults. He is saying, "*Look at me, I need you.*" The more he is ignored, the more he is likely to increase his demands.

When faced with a child who appears to be "attention seeking" the question to ask yourself is, "Who does this child want attention from and what do they want attention for?"

Communicating by projecting feelings

So why can it be so difficult to respond to a demanding child warmly? As anyone who has held a crying baby knows, babies communicate by projecting feelings, they make the adult feel what they are feeling. Troubled children often do the same, and so the attention seeking, needy child may make the playworker feel as irritable and helpless as they are feeling themselves. No wonder the adult is then left feeling that nothing works with that particular child.

If you ask yourself "How does this child make me feel?" it will give you some understanding of how the child might be feeling, regardless of how they are behaving. Once you recognise how they feel it will help you to respond to their behaviour. We need to also hold in mind the difference between containment and cure. The aim of good childcare is not to make bad feelings disappear but to help a child manage them.

How do we know which children to worry about?

Disruptive and disturbing behaviour also helps us to understand which children we should be worried about. The disruptive child still has the hope that out there is an adult who will certainly hear and take note of their anxieties. Much more worrying is the quiet and withdrawn child who may have given up on such a hope. These children can often be overlooked because they are not disrupting the group or demanding adults' attention.

* * *

Understanding children's behaviour as communication is no soft option in child management. Children need clear, firm boundaries throughout their childhood. If we show children that we understand how they feel, and that we can help them to find a better way of communicating how they feel, then they learn not only how to get their needs met, but also to respect themselves and other people.

How we view children's behaviour colours our reaction to it. I will also explore in this book how naughtiness is very much a matter of how a way of behaviour is construed. Any two playworkers may understand the same child as "a little rascal" or "a very naughty child". The difference between these two descriptions is that a little rascal is likely to inspire affection in adults and be treated leniently, but a naughty child is much more likely to make adults want to punish him and to be distant from him. The little rascal may get a kinder response from adults and may feel closer to adults, but he may not learn a more effective way of communicating his needs. For example, he may learn to rely upon being charmingly defiant—very effective for a five year old, less so for a twelve year old. So the child seen as naughty faces an even bigger muddle—he is likely to feel rejected by adults just at the time he needs to feel close.

* * *

I hope you will share my interest in the difficulties children pose for adults. They make us think, remember and associate, and in doing so, they provide us with very good tools for understanding them.

Playworkers share with teachers the fact that they are working with children in groups. We should remember that it is a strange experience for children to be in a peer group—such groups always occur outside the home; at home siblings are older or younger than the child. Additionally the parental couple is expanded from two to a number of carers.

While playworkers have considerably more opportunities for working with individual children within the group, they share a teacher's main obligation, which is to preserve the group. I hope this book will help playworkers (and also teachers and parents) to understand the paradox of children's behaviour, and that it will also provide constructive ideas for helping children to understand that their behaviour has to be acceptable to the group if they are to be allowed to remain in club.

PART ONE:
PLAYWORKERS, CHILDREN
AND BEHAVIOUR

ACTING THE PART: HOW CLUB IS LIKE, AND UNLIKE, THE FAMILY

Playworkers are in a good position to free a child from a restrictive role they have adopted due to their family dynamics

Children are never simply themselves. They carry with them all sorts of thoughts and ideas about themselves inherited from family life, particularly from their role in the family. Conflict is inevitable in families and in order to survive, all families have to find their own particular way of managing tensions. Often this is done unconsciously by family members taking on roles like "the clever one", or "the pretty one", for example.

Children often absorb their family role as an identity. Sometimes this is not a problem—the family survives and the child functions. The risk is when a child believes the family role is their only way of being, the only version of themselves that other people will find lovable and acceptable. A child can bring its family role to both school and club life, in that they may behave in club in the way they behave at home. Children at club should be feeling free to experiment with what they have learned about themselves in the family. For this reason, playworkers need to be aware of when it is appropriate to reinforce a family role and when it might be in the child's interests for club to offer the child an alternative way of being themselves.

Let us think about three frequently observed family roles: The sensible child, the scapegoat and the troublemaker.

The sensible child

Sensible children like nine year old Tom can be a boon. Mature, cheerful, willing, reliable, efficient; they are a natural choice to be given responsibilities. But sometimes sensible children can find their role a strain. Recently Tom's playworker had noticed a change in him. He seemed less good humoured and somewhat reluctant about his tasks at club. He seemed to be a avoiding other children. One day, Tom drew a picture of a mediaeval castle with three girls playing in the grounds. A soldier on horseback was riding away from the castle, another soldier paraded the turrets. Tom explained that the soldier riding away was the "war knight"—he had "*gone off to have fun at battle.*" The other soldier was the "guard knight"—left at home to look after the women and children. "*And he's fed up,*" added Tom.

Tom's father worked away from home several days a week, sometimes for longer. "*You are the man of the house now, look after your mum and sisters,*" he used to instruct Tom as he left for work. Tom's picture showed how burdened he felt by this well meaning, but totally impossible request. He was the fed up "guard knight" watching his father ride off to have fun. He had taken on the role of "the sensible one" to please his parents but in adopting this pseudo maturity he was missing out on the joys of being a little boy.

Tom's club workers realised that they had to respond to him by freeing him from responsibilities in club. Club had to be a place where he could be a carefree child. They realised that because he was so reliable they had fallen into the trap of reinforcing his pseudo maturity by giving him special jobs to do in club.

The sensible child as peacemaker

When eleven year old Josie arrived in club, her playworkers were impressed by her maturity. She was keen and eager to take on responsibilities which she carried out reliably and efficiently. She was also very skilled at intervening as a peacemaker in other children's rows and conflicts. But several months later, they were worried: at times, Josie seemed over helpful to the point of being irritating. She would follow club workers round asking if they had any jobs she would like to do or repeatedly enquiring whether "*I should do this or that.*" They also noticed she often tried to divert her playworker when he was managing children's conflicts, offering her version of events, whether she was involved or not.

Josie's parents had a volatile relationship, often erupting into violent rows. Josie had taken on the role of peacemaker in the family. Her mother gave a typical example. After a row one evening, she asked Josie to tell her father, "*Supper is ready—and has been for ten minutes.*" Her father replied tersely, "*I heard her the first time . . . tell her I'm on my way.*" Josie repeated the message but then provoked an aggressive argument with her younger brother, at which point both parents told her off soundly. We can think of Josie as a child trying to keep the peace between her parents. Unconsciously, she had diverted their conflict from each other onto herself. She would rather her parents were shouting at her than shouting at each other.

15

Children like Josie may make excellent monitors but may develop a phobic attitude to conflict. They have sacrificed their own needs and desires in order to avoid conflict and may grow up not only as "people pleasers" but also quite terrified of an argument developing in her presence. Josie's club workers offered her a space to be open about her anxieties and to find healthier ways of managing them. Initially Josie found this difficult and she seemed hurt and rejected when, for example, her explanations of what might have gone on between two other children were firmly but kindly rejected if she had not been involved in the incident. Her club workers would remind her *"This is not your problem, Josie, there is no need for you to try and make peace."* However, gradually it became clear that she felt relieved from the heavy burden of always having to mediate in other people's arguments.

The Scapegoat

Scapegoats are very important people. They help the rest of us to avoid our fears and anxieties. Think about Josie— her parents resolved their own conflict by uniting to scapegoat Josie.

Tim is a twelve year old who found it difficult to make friends. When he did have a friend, there was always conflict. He would try to get his friend to "gang up" with him against others, causing a split in the group. And he did the same with the staff, frequently reporting inaccurately to one playworker that another had given him permission to do something. He was also divisive, for example, telling one staff member that her colleague had complained, *"You didn't make us put the art things away properly."*

This "splitting" is a common phenomenon in children whose parents knowingly draw them into their conflicts. It is, of course, inevitable that all children are drawn into parental conflict at some time or other, but that is a different situation to when parents decide to involve their children. For example, when Tim's father arrived home too late for his mother to go to her evening class, she said, "*Well, Tim was very disappointed you weren't here to help with his maths, weren't you, Tim?*" inviting Tim to join her in attacking his father. The result was that Tim was growing up with the idea that someone always has to be left out. In club, he worked hard to ensure that it was not him but, of course, his attempts to scapegoat other people tended to leave him isolated.

It was hard work for club workers to help Tim to realise that it was possible to be friends with more than one person at a time. They did so not only by talking with Tim individually but also by having general group discussions on how it felt to be left out and also what it meant to have friends.

The positive scapegoat

Tim's parents used Tim as ammunition against each other but sometimes families scapegoat one member in a more positive way, such as the "success" of the family. Megan, bright and attractive, was such a child. There seemed to be no area in which she didn't shine—academia, sport, music. Holiday club began the day after her school's prize day. Her playworker was surprised to see Megan looking downcast. "*Well done, Megan,*" she greeted her, "*I hear you won four prizes.*" To her surprise, Megan burst into tears

17

and eventually explained that whilst she had been pleased to win her prizes, she felt under pressure because, "... *now I'll always have to win.*"

We need to be watchful of the successful child because the risk for them is that they may be allowing everyone else to fail! By being the "successful one" in the family, Megan was assuaging her parents' anxieties about being "good enough" parents; the fantasy being that if one child in the family was doing well, it proved they were succeeding as parents in some way. In another sense, Megan was relieving the pressure on her siblings to succeed. They were more able to take life at their own pace because Megan was successful. The problem for Megan was that she was growing up feeling she was only loveable if she succeeded. It was not that her parents had meant to give her that message but Megan was obviously conscious of how much her success meant to them.

In club, Megan needed reassurance that she was equally as acceptable, whether failing or succeeding. Her club workers tried to focus their praise more on aspects of her personality and qualities than her achievements. Children like Megan may find a great relief in being allowed to fail.

The troublemaker

Troublemakers are also often working very hard for both their family and for club. Remember how Josie "made" trouble to rescue her parents? Chris was a ten year old who was always in trouble, at home and away. His playworkers were relieved on the rare occasions he didn't attend: "*The group is so different when he's not here, there's just no trouble at all.*" His parents echoed this sentiment at home, "*It's so peaceful when he's not here,*" said his mother.

Children often take on the role of troublemaker in families where there is something difficult and hard to manage creaking away in everyday life. There were huge tensions in Chris's parents' marriage. It became easy to call the hard-to-manage thing in the family "Chris"—a persona he carried into club.

"*None of the others behave like that,*" moaned his play leader. Well, the other children didn't need to make trouble, because Chris could always be relied on to do it for them. They may have felt equally disgruntled about club rules or activities organised, but they didn't protest because they knew that Chris would always kick up a fuss.

Troublemakers help us to avoid dealing with our own conflicts. So a child like Chris, often accused of disrupting a group, may actually be looking after the group. Chris needed help to step out of his family role and to fight only the battles that belonged to him.

Club is like home and unlike home. Playworkers are like a parent and unlike a parent. Unconsciously, children are constantly asking, *"Is club a good enough substitute for my parents?"* and *"Is club an interesting new world?"* The great advantage of playworkers is that they are not parents. You are new adults who may allow children to experiment with substituting an "acquired personality" for the experience of being an authentic individual with their own thoughts, needs and special things to say.

GROWING UP: THE PRIMARY SCHOOL YEARS

Working out where children are on the physical and cognitive continuum can enhance understanding during the pre-teenage years

Both adults and children attach great importance to age in childhood. "*How old are you?*" is often our opening question. "*Seven but I'm nearly eight,*" is typical of their telling replies. While adults perceive little difference in a year in their own age dramatic developmental changes take place in a year in a child's life and no more rapidly than in the club years.

Seven year olds are still very much children preoccupied with school, play and their place in the family. As they approach Year 4 they will increase their steps to independence by taking more interest in the world outside home. They may mimic teenagers, talking about pop stars, discos, love and sex but are equally as likely to believe in Father Christmas and the Tooth Fairy.

By Year 7 children may be clearly adolescent in their ways and interests. They are much more focussed on life outside the home. However, there will still be marked differences in their behaviour and teen behaviour. For example, at a social gathering they are likely to choose to be with the children, whereas, of course, a teenager would want to be with the adults.

It can be arbitrary to divide children strictly into groups as child development happens in a very broad spectrum, but having a rough idea of where a child is physically and cognitively can help us to understand them as people.

We can also understand what attending club may mean to them. Historically, the club years have always been known as "latency", a relatively stable, calm period when sexual curiosity goes underground and children are consolidating what they know. However, in this modern era, childhood is changing and this age group is becoming more challenging and turbulent. It is now more realistic to think of latency as the 7–9 year old group and the 9–12 year olds as the "betweenage" stage.

Mood swings and the beginning of puberty

Seven year olds are fine tuning their coordination to master activities such as playing sports and musical instruments. They begin to take a pride in their own skills and abilities and to be aware of how they differ from those of their friends.

Young children describe themselves concretely, e.g., *"I'm Marcus and I'm five."* Now they are also more likely to describe their skills and abilities. For example, *"I'm Marcus and I'm good at football."*

By nine, they will feel that they know themselves and will feel comfortable and confident in their bodies. All this is about to change with the onset of the betweenage years.

Studies from Great Ormond Street Hospital show that puberty may begin as young as at eight years old for both girls and boys. Sex hormones, especially in girls, begin to increase gradually in the body from about seven years old. Although the levels are not large enough to stimulate physical changes such as breasts or pubic hair developing, they do affect the brain, causing mood swings. Professor Peter Hindmarsh likens the situation for the betweenager as not unlike that for a woman in the first three months of pregnancy, who may feel awful but appears normal and it is not until the pregnancy is showing that she receives the sympathy she needs. Children get their sympathy when symptoms like acne, for example, begin to appear, which is unlikely to be as young as eight or nine years old.

I have highlighted elsewhere (Clifford-Poston, 2005) how by nine years old, children who are still pre-pubertal will be aware of and curious about teenage bodies and all that they signify. We can think of betweenagers as experiencing a crisis of body ambition; what kind of body do I want? What kind of body will I have? How will my body compare with that of my friends?

In contrast to the growing competence and confidence of a seven year old, a betweenager may be struggling with a loss of self-image. Their agile, coordinated, even graceful child bodies are being replaced with ones that are not only awkward and clumsy but also seem alien to them. They may worry about the contrast between their bodies and the glamorous and sexy teenage bodies they see all around them. They may also feel their body doesn't really belong to them any more and face the dilemma of dressing it up in teenage clothes or returning to comfortable latency by wearing inappropriately child-like outfits or a unisex uniform of tracksuits, jeans and t-shirts.

Working out morality

In the club years, children begin to change the way they think. On the whole, 7–9 years olds tend to live in a black and white world where things are right or wrong, fair or not fair. Their morality and sense of values will be what they have been taught by adults with no shades of grey— one eight year old girl wanted to sell her toys at a boot sale because, "*All* the children in Africa are dying."

They tend to take language literally and understand words as they apply to their experience. A seven year old was very perplexed when he saw a sign "Self drive cars." He had witnessed many arguments between his mother and father as his father complained of his mother "riding the clutch". He couldn't understand why his parents had to argue about the driving if cars could drive themselves!

In contrast, betweenagers are beginning to develop the capacity for abstract thought, resulting in them questioning all sorts of issues. A seven year old may help to raise money for victims of the latest crisis but a betweenager will be beginning to think also about the causes of the crisis and man's part in them; they are beginning to work out their own morality and what they believe in.

They may become fervent about topics such as human suffering or animal welfare and try hard to convert everyone else to their views. Betweenagers may not have a sophisticated sense of nuances and so may carry their views to extremes and their fervour may lead them into danger. Two eleven year old girls told how they had seen a man abusing his dog and had stopped to tell him they would report him to the RSPCA!

In many ways they may represent our conscience. Once, two eleven year olds arrived at my door selling chocolate muffins in aid of the *Tsunami* disaster. They explained the muffins were £5 each. When I could not contain my astonishment, one of them fixed me with a steely look and said, "*They* so have nothing."

Betweenagers are also anxious. They realise they are losing the seemingly uncomplicated world of childhood and adults no longer seem to know everything.

One of the biggest changes playworkers will notice between the latency and the betweenage child is that betweenagers are much more argumentative. They sound out their beliefs by delighting in practicing their newly discovered skill of arguing with adults.

Crucial to be cool

Children's play develops rapidly in latency. Reading and writing open up a whole new world to them including, for example, board games, through which they learn to appreciate and understand rules and procedures such as taking turns.

Board games are popular with this age group, and this is interesting as board games do not involve passion; children may become passionate about winning or losing but the games themselves are clear cut: there is a definite beginning, goal, rules about how to reach that goal, and a winner. There are no shades of grey, they are "contained" games.

Latency children are also contained. They have grown beyond the passions of toddlerhood and have not yet developed as adolescents. Their passions are being metabolised underground during latency. They are contained in a sense that, on the whole, they can bear their own anxiety and frustration. They no longer need to communicate it in temper tantrums like a toddler. Nor do they feel they have to act out worries like a teenager.

Toddlers and teenagers are driven internally to do something when they are anxious, latency children do not need to do anything. They develop greater awareness of other people's feelings, which enhances their tolerance and understanding. However, they are still learning to put themselves in other people's shoes and friendships at this age may be characterised by spats and petty quarrels.

The betweenage years bring a huge change in social and emotional relationships. Betweenagers are clearer about their ambivalence towards adults than the latency child, who remains dependent on adults' approval. Betweenagers do and do not want to please adults. At any age children want to be popular with their peers, for a betweenager it begins to be crucial to be "in the cool group." Their desire to be seen as "cool" reflects their growing struggles with their self-image and identity.

I have written elsewhere (Clifford-Poston, 2005) that friendships also change considerably. They are less likely to be orchestrated by parents and will have a best friend. They are beginning to be aware of subtle differences in friendships; one sad nine year old girl reported, "*I get invited to the parties but nobody asks me round . . . like for tea or anything.*" Like many betweenagers, she felt she could only be either "in the cool group" or "without mates."

Parents and family now take second place to friends. Betweenagers are preoccupied with developing their life outside home to the point where the demands of home life may even feel intrusive on their privacy.

Betweenagers are, of course, beginning to think about sexual relationships. Unlike teenagers, they are preoccupied more with the romance of sex than engaging in sex. For many, sexuality means beginning to see the opposite sex as opposite, as different and potentially exciting.

'Going out' doesn't necessarily mean going anywhere. For many betweenage girls, "liking" boys may have nothing

25

to do with sex or even kissing, while betweenage boys may often see girls as a kind of "girl-boy," a different kind of a companion on the computer.

Cooperate or contempt

There is a big difference between caring for a young child and looking after an almost independent one. The former is likely to be cooperative and eager to please, and to enjoy what you have to offer, while the latter may be dismissive and even contemptuous. It can be difficult not to take such behaviour personally or to vilify the betweenager because of it.

We need to appreciate that betweenagers and latency children are using club in different ways. For the younger child, club may be an exciting bridge from home to the wider world. For betweenagers, it may be a place to practice all kinds of versions of themselves not acceptable at home.

We also need to hold in mind that however independent a child may be becoming, they are still dependent (as indeed we all are). They may be able to do more and more for themselves and increasing their ability to care for themselves but they are still dependant on their parents and the other adults in the world around them.

The role of club workers for this age group is to help the child feel that their independence is becoming more and more viable.

TOYS OR BOYS:
BETWEENAGERS

Remember how you irritated your parents as a teenager? Well, now it is your turn to deal with the perplexing behaviour of a new phenomena—the betweenagers

Ollie, aged ten, swaggered into the first day of holiday club tuned into his i-Pod. His hands thrust into his pockets, his hips swaying and a bored, if a little anxious, look on his face as he sauntered over to Meg and Amy. They were sporting matching crop tops and mini skirts and earnestly trying on each other's oversized sunglasses.

They turned as Ollie approached and giggled, *"You look well fit."* They were interrupted by Ollie's playworker calling him to register. The girls tossed their heads and looked away sulkily. Ollie curled his lip, stared at the floor and begun to scuff imaginary dirt. *"Just look at that,"* said Ollie's playworker, *"they are just like teenagers at ten now."*

Childhood is changing. Children are maturing physically much earlier; it is not uncommon for year 5 or even year 4 children to have entered puberty. They are also much more exposed to, and influenced by, the media. Discos and make-over parties have become the norm to celebrate birthdays. We have a whole generation of children who have never played "pin-the-tail-on-the-donkey." But these children are not teenagers.

Ollie's playworker is both right and wrong. They are "like teenagers" but they are also "not like teenagers".

Hovering between the passing world of childhood and the risky world of adolescence, they are "betweenagers." They have their own music, culture and fashions. They are carefully researched and targeted by the media. Designer clothes and mobile phones are the "must haves" of daily life.

Betweenagers are not just younger teenagers. They may look and sound like teenagers but they have very different preoccupations and concerns. Betweenagers are playing with the idea of being a teenager. They are trying to find out what it is like to be a teenager. For them, the mobile phones and designer fashions are an extension of toys. Many still play with toys as enthusiastically as they learn the latest dance. They want adults to watch "the play" as they experiment with being grown up—and not interrupt. They want adults to take them seriously, but they also want adults to know this is a play! So how does all this impact on out-of-school clubs?

The right age?

Playworkers may feel confused by these "teenage children." At one time the worst a playworker might fear from this age group was the odd act of deliberate defiance or a spontaneous "bit of cheek". Both could be easily managed firmly—and swiftly. Now many playworkers struggle with anxieties about underage smoking, drinking and sexual behaviour. Part of your dilemma in working with betweenagers is reviewing what is the "right age" for these things? Do we rely on research, biological facts . . . or what?

Betweenagers seem to be an age group where facts don't work. The risk for adults is that we simply stop thinking behind a wall of "they're not old enough."

Playworkers were initially amused as Ollie, Meg and Amy hovered on the edge of the group, seemingly absorbed in their own world. But when any encouragement to join in was met with a shrug and "*It's boring*", the charm wore off, for betweenagers are, above all, irritating.

"*Ollie used to be such a sweetie, he still can be,*" said his playworker, "*but he's developing a real attitude . . . I get quite fed up with him . . . I never used to be . . .*"

This was an interesting comment. As children grow up, we find our responses to them change. What is cute and endearing at three, can be annoying and repulsive at ten. So, the first way we know children are changing is by the change in the way we respond to them, the way they make us feel about them. Betweenagers make us feel a bit helpless, powerless, as they change from being co-operative and responsive to being sullen, if not rude, and uncooperative. They can make us feel confused—do we react to them as children or as adolescents? It is unclear.

What is clear, however, is that if we react to betweenagers as though they were adolescents, our confusion is increased. Ollie, Meg and Amy's behaviour was clearly telling the playworkers they could amuse themselves better than the playworkers could amuse them. Such rejection can be hard to take, particularly when you have been viewed previously as a source of all fun.

Being irritating is an interesting communication from a betweenager. We can think of being irritating as a way of frustrating someone or something—so being irritated by a betweenager is a sign that you are in touch with them. When Ollie and co irritated their playworkers by not joining in, were they simply not listening? Were they saying their agenda was more important than the adults? Or was this a way of being sexually provocative? We could think of being irritating as a betweenager's way of finding out how adults will respond to something before they do it. Unconsciously, they may have been asking, how will the grown ups respond if we behave sexually together? And this is part of the confusion.

Betweenagers are unlike teenagers in a very significant way. For teenagers, sex is on the agenda, even if it is denied! Betweenagers are children who are clearly beginning to be adult. So were Ollie, Meg and Amy flirting? Were they just being companionable? The problem is that no one knows, least of all Ollie, Meg and Amy. A very interesting thing happened. By lunchtime that day, Ollie had discarded his i-Pod and the girls their sunglasses as they enthusiastically joined in a game of cricket. "*They're just kids really*," commented a play leader as they watched them running about with the other children. Teenagers have "put away childish things", but for betweenagers toys and games may be equally as important as the trappings of the teenage world. This is a complex situation for a playworker to manage, for the likelihood is that all those scenarios were being enacted simultaneously.

Managing betweenagers

- Remember what you were like as you approached your teens. Faced with difficult behaviour we find hard to manage, we all too easily forget what we were like at a similar age. You can't remember being a betweenager, of course, because this is a newly defined group. However, although the facts may be different—you may not have wanted a make-over party at aged eight—the feelings are the same. You too were once irritating and confusing to adults! It can be useful to reflect on what the adults did that was helpful and unhelpful.

- Remember, you might be the first generation of playworkers having to deal with betweenagers. Much betweenagers' behaviour is aimed at needling adults. It is about trying to find out what the adult is made of, how firm and resolute are the boundaries, and where the authority figures are in the room. If you have time in a busy club to monitor how the betweenager is making you feel, it will give you a clue on the best way to respond. Ollie's play leader felt "*like losing my rag with them,*" in other words setting firm boundaries. So were Ollie, Meg and Amy unconsciously asking the play leader to make them join in—to protect them from themselves?

- It is not always easy to think on your feet in the hurly-burly of club life. You can learn just as much by reflecting on your impulsive behaviour. What happened just before you "lost your rag"? What were you feeling and why did those feelings make you respond the way you did? Remember this is new territory for us all.

- Try to hold in mind the differences between teenagers and this age group. Betweenagers are children acting like teenagers. Betweenagers enjoy confrontations; on the whole adults do not. Whilst betweenagers need firm, clear boundaries, they also need flexibility, or at least the illusion of flexibility. So it may be helpful never to give your bottom line right away when you are managing a betweenager. If you know you are going to insist they join in, you might want to lead up to that rather than state it right away. There is all the difference in the world between "*you have to join in or*

> *go home"* and *"what do you need to do or finish before you join in . . .?"*

Betweenagers are a new phenomenon. They don't know what's going on and so it is not surprising adults are puzzled. If you remember that betweenagers are experimenting with an enigmatic state you will gain confidence by understanding that your own sense of confusion and not knowing what to do is part of the process—the process in which adults care enough about children to let them become themselves.

SCREAMING POINT:
STRESS IN CHILDCARE

If stress is acted on it can help us to find better ways to manage our work

A young mother was complaining to her older colleague in holiday club about the challenges of balancing her home and work commitments. *"It's all so stressful ,"* she sighed, *"how did you manage it . . .?"* The older woman thought for a moment and then replied, *"I don't think I thought about it, I was just too busy, I didn't have time to think about being stressed . . ."*

No one is immune from stress and maybe this is why the word has become so popular. It is also possible, however, that stress is a word being used nowadays with many different meanings. The playworker who said she *"didn't have time to be stressed"* probably found it just as difficult to balance work and home commitments but she is describing it very differently. She was, she says, *"just busy."* So what is the difference between ordinary "busy-ness," hard work and stress?

When stress starts

From time to time I visit a club which has been especially successful with children with special educational needs. Eventually, they were asked if they would increase their places for such children from four to eight. The staff reacted with mixed feelings, pleased that their work was being recognised but anxious about the extra workload. By the time I was present at a team meeting two weeks later, people were feeling angry and frustrated. Most of the staff were afraid they wouldn't be able to cope and felt the decision had been foisted upon them. They described feeling "stressed" by the change in policy. This was interesting as they were all aware they had the necessary skills, training and experience to cope with the extra children. We began to brainstorm exactly what they thought would be "stressful" about the increase in numbers. Interestingly, they produced a list of practical "what ifs . . ." which illustrated how most of the staff were feeling anxious rather than stressed about the change in policy.

Stress occurs when we begin to feel anxious and we usually express our anxiety as a fear of being expected to do more than we feel capable of doing. Stress also occurs when people feel angry and frustrated about lack of power and resources. So when we are feeling stressed, it may be helpful to ask *"What am I anxious/angry about?"* and, *"What can I do about it?"* This can be empowering because when we identify the resources available to us, we can prompt ourselves to find better ways of managing our work. The alternative may be to just helplessly think about being stressed.

Why we choose to work with children

People working with children seem particularly vulnerable to stress although they usually enjoy their jobs. Why should this be?

On the whole, work with children is underpaid and relatively undervalued. A lack of resources and sometimes poor working conditions can be daily reminders to practitioners that their skills go unrecognised. Sometimes this makes it difficult for us to hold onto the belief that our work is worthwhile and this can make us feel anxious and depressed, which we may then misconstrue as stress. For many practitioners currently these feelings have been exacerbated by the number of policy changes in early years work.

Other stresses are more subtle. Many people who work with children do so from a sense of vocation. They probably knew from a very early age that working with children was what they wanted to do. They may have been influenced by family traditions; for example, it is common to find several teachers in several generations of one family, but the overriding motivation is often vocation.

Working with children may also be a "remedy" for a difficult childhood. Some people may feel, quite rightly, that they have a heightened awareness of what it is like to be a child. They may also have a fantasy that by helping other children to have a good childhood, they are somehow eradicating the pain of their own. A club worker whose own childhood lacked affection was particularly affectionate towards the children in her care because she knew they needed it and enjoyed it but also as a way of cuddling the deprived baby inside herself. She knew intuitively what children needed because she knew what she had missed.

High expectations

This sense of vocation and the need to give others a good childhood can lead people working with children to have overly high expectations of themselves in their work. Marie, an experienced playworker, was embarrassed when her friends frequently turned to her for help in managing their own children. On one occasion, having run the gamut of her suggestions, her friend said irritably, *"You're the expert, you should know what to do with him!"*

Being thought to be "good with children" brings its own stresses. Marie immediately felt that she should produce some magic which she couldn't and consequently felt deskilled, hopeless and stressed. Her expectation of herself was that she should be able to offer her friend some sound, practical advice which would be effective. She was stressed, not so much by her failure to come up with workable management skills, but by her own expectation that she should be able to do so. And we could argue that that very expectation of herself was paralysing her skills.

Staff may also find the expectations of parents of children at club can cause stress. Parents may perceive practitioners as experts who can fill the holes in their parenting skills and stresses arise when their expectations seem thwarted. If parents are critical or disagree with practitioners over club practice then this can also cause tensions. In such situations club workers may do best to take the line, *"Look, we don't have to agree about this, but we both want what is best for the children."*

Sharing children's pain

Children's feelings are very powerful by virtue of their primitive nature. Babies and toddlers tell adults how they feel by making the adults feel the same, as anyone who has held a crying baby knows! To some extent this projection continues throughout life; we have probably all had the experience of the mood of a lively, happy group sinking when joined by one depressed personality.

Our self-image, the way we perceive ourselves as good or bad, lovable or unlovable, is a reflection of how we are treated by other people. So if a child has suffered a destructive or painful experience within the family, they may be likely to bring that to their club workers in the form of difficult or disruptive behaviour. Staff may feel helpless and angry when faced with a child who seems both disturbed and disturbing, and this is not surprising because the child is making you feel what they feel, i.e., angry and helpless. Paradoxically, it is when we feel most at a loss with a child that we are likely to be most connected to them. Understanding how a child feels is the best route to successful managing. So faced with a difficult child it is worth asking, *"How does this child make me feel?"* By doing so, you may once again turn stress into a resource.

When working with groups of children we are constantly receiving their feelings, consciously or unconsciously. We all know a lot more happens in club than is seen to be said or done. We may well feel stressed at the end of the day by the myriad of emotions projected onto us. The secret here is to learn to recognise which are our own feelings and which are those of the child.

It is impossible to work with children and not have our own early childhood emotions stirred up. Adults working with children have to share the children's feelings in order to understand them, but if we cannot disassociate them from our own feelings then we may end up being very critical of parents. This is particularly true where practitioners have had a difficult childhood themselves. When staff understand their anger with their own parents, they are free to develop compassion and understanding for the children's parents to whom they can become a valuable resource.

37

How to avoid stress

- Take time to assimilate the feelings you absorb during your working day. Try to avoid filling breaks with preparation or meetings.
- Briefly reflect on what happened during the day, but try not to dwell on it. Doing your work properly will mean that it seeps into your private life, but equally you are not doing your work properly if you allow it to invade your private life on a daily basis.
- Do not take on more work than you can handle. Being overloaded is likely to make you re-active rather than pro-active, so the children will not get what they need. You are responsible for an individual child professionally, not for the child's whole life. Unless the child is in danger, your professional role is to help them negotiate the difficulties of their childhood, not to take them away.
- Avoid impossibly high, self-induced demands. No child needs a perfect practitioner, only one that is "good enough."
- If you feel overloaded, ask for help. This is a sign of maturity, not weakness. Talking an issue through with a colleague or friend may help to put it in perspective and is likely to lead to some more clear management strategies.
- Keep a careful balance between home and work so you keep the sense of fun that children need most.
- Be realistic rather than idealistic about what you have to offer to children.

YOU REALLY GOT ME!
THE CHILD WHO GETS
UNDER YOUR SKIN

When a certain child particularly
irritates you, ask yourself why you
feel this way and what the child
might be trying to tell you.

A group of playworkers running a holiday club were
discussing nine year old Peter, a polite, well behaved boy
who seemed rather isolated from his peers. "*He's always
alongside a group, never in the group,*" said one. There was
a murmur of agreement and a moment of reflective silence
before another burst out, "*Oh, I know it's an awful thing
to say, but I'm not surprised, I can't stand that kid, he really
gets under my skin.*"

When we choose to work with children we do so with
a degree of pride in our ability to relate to and understand
them. We can feel at best disconcerted, and at worst guilty,
when we find ourselves irritated by or disinterested in
a child. So what do we mean when we say a child "gets
under our skin?" Usually, this is when we find ourselves
responding to them in a way we don't really want or like.
The child may make us feel we have to respond to them
instantly, or they may haunt us in the sense that we find
ourselves thinking about them very frequently, sometimes
constantly. Sometimes "getting under my skin" can mean
we are drawn to a child and we feel we want to be more
involved with them; often it means we find we want to
protect ourselves from contact with the child. Peter's

playworker admitted she was so irritated by Peter she tried to avoid him, "*There's just something about him . . . he's so smarmy with it . . . it makes my flesh creep.*" She found it very difficult to think about Peter and what his behaviour might mean. Interestingly, Peter did not have the same effect on her colleagues, but they all agreed that another child, eight year old Marie, got under all their skins with her immature behaviour and by talking in a baby voice. "*I think she thinks it's cute,*" said one playworker, "*it's not, it's just really annoying.*" So why is it that some children get under everyone's skin and others just impact on one or two members of staff?

"Getting under your skin" as a communication

I have already talked about how babies communicate by projecting feelings—they tell the adult how they feel by making the adult feel what they are feeling. And this carries on into childhood. We have been thinking about how children, by adults' standards, have limited ways of telling us when they have a worry, and how if they haven't got the language or if they don't understand their own confusion, then they use behaviour as a communication. Peter behaved in a courteous and almost "goody-goody" manner but his playworker wasn't impressed by his politeness. Indeed, she felt almost aggressive towards him. Of course, all children use getting under their parents' skin as a way of bonding with them; they are trying to get as close to their parents as possible in any way possible. But when the child gets under other people's skin, we need to think about what might be going on.

Peter was the youngest of three children and the only boy. His much older sisters were clever and competent and, as emerged later, he felt they took up most of his busy parents' attention. Peter admitted to feeling a little left out in the family, pointing out pertinently, "*My sisters never had to go to holiday club, my mum didn't work then.*" It was not surprising that this resentment made him feel jealous of his sisters but he was afraid to show his anger in the family for fear it might make him even less acceptable to his parents. So he protected himself and everyone else from his rage by being excessively well-behaved and polite. But feelings have a way of seeping out into sensitive and receptive adults around a child—Peter was making his playworker feel his anger so she could understand him.

Often the child who gets under our skin is the one we are most likely to be able to understand and help. Unconsciously, Peter had sensed his playworker had something to offer him, and indeed she had because she too had struggled with envy and rage as a child. Paradoxically, the children (and adults!) we most dislike are often those who remind us of some abject or unpleasant part of ourselves we would rather forget. Peter and his playworker had got into a muddle in their relationship. Unconsciously, he had identified her as someone who knew how it felt to be him; she, on the other hand, didn't want to be reminded of some of the pain of her own childhood. Peter had less impact on other staff because he was not projecting a part of himself into them in the same way.

The child who gets under everyone's skin

Let us now think about Marie who affected all the adults in the same way. Marie was the eldest of five children, there was less than a year between her and her younger sister. Her mother was puzzled by her immature behaviour in club as at home, "... *she is very grown up and a good help with the little ones.*" Marie never used a "baby voice" at home.

When children come to club they bring with them an unconscious expectation of how the adults will treat them. They base this expectation on how their parents have treated them. The child with authoritarian parents and the child with *laissez faire* parents may approach their playworkers with very different attitudes. Marie's parents had always expected her to be more responsible and grown up than was possible for a small child. In a sense her "baby needs" had not been met as other babies had arrived in the family so quickly. We can understand her babyish behaviour at club as her way of warning her playworkers not to expect too much of her and to allow her to be a small child in club. She had cast them in the role of demanding parents before they had all had a chance to get to know each other. Marie was a worrying (and worried!) child in the sense that getting under everyone's skin was a sign of her desperation. However, it was also a sign that she still believed there were adults around who would listen to and understand her. Indeed, once both Marie and Peter's playworkers began to respond to how they felt, rather than to the way they behaved, they became much less troubling. Marie's playworkers were careful not to give her any responsibilities in club, and as Peter's playworker was able to give him some individual time and attention, he slowly became more ready to show her his anger and unhappiness.

When we want to do more

Sometimes a child may get under our skin in the sense that we find ourselves always wanting to do that little bit more for them. This is when we need to think about the difference between really liking and understanding a child and the child who gets under our skin to such an extent that we find ourselves doing unusual things. We may feel we need to be in contact with this child outside club or buy them presents or pay for them to go on trips, for example. Such a child may feel desperate in their belief that adults can't listen to or won't understand them. They may try to fuse themselves into us in an adhesive way, making us feel we have to help them or disaster will happen; this, of course, is exactly how they feel.

Managing the child who gets under your skin

- Ask yourself "how does this child really make me feel?"
- Ask yourself if it is possible that the child feels the same but needs to deny it.
- Ask yourself who this child reminds you of and whether this memory could be colouring your response to the child?

- When you want to do more, pause and reflect on what you think you are actually doing by doing more, and whether or not you can achieve the same results in club.
- Remember, if a child gets under your skin, you are likely to have the potential to work well with them.

PART TWO:
STRESS AND WORRY

OUT OF PLACE: THE CHILD
WHO DOESN'T SETTLE

Some children may take more
time than others to settle into club
and it is important to find out
the reasons why

Club is a fun place and most children settle quickly and
smoothly into the routine and activities, but now and then
a child comes along who finds club difficult to manage;
they may be aggressive and disruptive or, at the other
extreme, tearful, withdrawn and clearly unhappy. In a way
this is not surprising: club isn't home and isn't school—
it's a third place for children to negotiate, and some
children take longer than others to do so.

The child who doesn't settle may be worried about
something, so the first question to ask should always be
"How settled is this child in school?" If they seem to
be coping with school well enough then the next stage is
to ask the parents if there is anything the child might be
worried about at home. However, we need to bear in mind
that a number of issues are going to influence a child's
capacity to feel at ease in club.

What does being in club mean to
the child?

At one level we all know club is where children go while
their parents are working or otherwise occupied. But it may

also be a place a child might choose to go to, to be with other children and to do interesting activities. These are conscious, thought-about reasons why children are in club. But our experiences also have internal meanings for us and from which we deduce unconscious, not thought-about explanations for our life events and experiences.

Let us think about eight year old Martin who attended after school club four evenings a week. Martin had never settled into club. He wasn't aggressive, but was always reluctant to join in and his playworkers found it difficult to find activities to excite or interest him. They had learned to coax and persuade him but inevitably at some point he would become distraught over what seemed to be a trivial matter, usually that he felt something was unfair or, as in one incident, that he had been dealt a raw deal by being given a table tennis bat with a crack in it. "*It's rubbish,*" he cried, "*I always get the rubbish,*" and he threw the bat down and strode off.

Martin had not chosen to attend club. He was the younger of three siblings and when he reached Year 3, his mother took a job outside the home for the first time, meaning she could no longer be at home at the end of the school day. Martin had been used to having his mother to himself after school for an hour before his older brothers came home. Now he had to attend club until one of his brothers collected him and took him home to await their mother's return.

Intellectually, Martin understood about mothers working, but emotionally he felt "*My mum's dumped me 'cos she likes her work.*" He was easily upset at club by anything that made him feel he was unworthy, like the damaged bat, because being given "a rubbish bat" spoke to his worst fears: that *he* was rubbish, i.e., unworthy of his mother's time and attention. To him it felt as though his mother would rather be at work than be with him.

In contrast was another eight year old, Stephen, who had begged his parents to let him go to club because his older brothers had so much fun there. Stephen experienced club as an exciting, creative space where he could both extend his peer relationships and learn new activities. At both a conscious and an unconscious level, children will always hold home experiences and club experiences together in their minds and how they are feeling about home will always colour how they settle into club.

What do transitions mean to the child?

"It's somewhere you go between school and home."

Club is a transitional world, lying as it does between school and home. Club aged children are usually secure in the world of home and in the world of school (and, of course, in their own world!). They have been in both for a long time, they know the "drill". For many, club is a space between home and school, a step into the wider, unknown world outside, but within the security of a familiar environment. Being allowed to stay on for club can be a signal that you are now a bit more grown up and independent.

Transitions are about letting go and moving forward. Stephen experienced club as a place where he could let go, albeit a little, of childhood and move forward into the world of his older siblings. *"It's a chance to be in a team!"* he described club excitedly.

But Martin was not ready to be in a team, he still needed more time with his mother before he was ready to move forward. So he experienced club as somewhere he didn't want to be, a no man's land between school (which he knew he had to attend) and home, where he longed to be. He couldn't get involved with club or enjoy any of the activities because he was preoccupied with not wanting to be there and feeling he *"wasn't anywhere . . . just in space . . . club hasn't got anything . . . not anything interesting."* Was it that club offered nothing interesting or that he was only interested in having time with his mother?

The transitional aspect of club resonates with this age group because, developmentally, they are in a state of transition. Physically, emotionally and intellectually they are preoccupied with moving from the world of childhood to the world of adolescence. Indeed we could think that how well a child copes in club may be a sign of how well they are coping with puberty.

How secure does a child feel?

"Well, Stephen's a much more confident child," said Martin's play leader as she tried to think about his behaviour, *"Martin seems so insecure."* The difference between a confident, secure child and one who seems both anxious and difficult to manage, is how they feel about themselves inside.

Stephen seemed reasonably sure that he was likeable and lovable and that the world outside home would welcome him and treat him well. We have already thought about how we gain this sense of good self-esteem by becoming closely emotionally attached to our parents or carers in infancy, who love us for who we are regardless of our appearance, skills and abilities. This close attachment leads us to identify with adults and want to grow up and acquire adult skills like reading and writing. It helps us to feel free to be curious about and eager to explore the world. Stephen was ready and curious, confident he could achieve similarly to his older siblings. He was carrying inside that good image of himself given to him by his parents' love and approval. He had also absorbed the experience of a "good parent" inside him who would be with him mentally and emotionally as he ventured into the world.

Martin, on the other hand, was what psychoanalyst John Bowlby would have described as "insecurely attached". His parenting had not been so reliable and consistent, and mentally he was always checking if his mother was there and loved him. This central preoccupation gave him little mental space to feel free to be curious about the welcoming excitements available at club. We can understand this as adults when we think about times when we have a major worry which takes over our life: we simply seem to be unable to concentrate on anything else.

Managing the child who doesn't settle

Put simply, at club Stephen felt held, Martin felt unheld. Children like Martin need their playworkers to help them to feel emotionally and physically contained and held in club. The following suggestions may provide guidance:

- In thinking about a child who doesn't settle, it is always worth trying to find out how they behave at other ordinary transitions of life, such as going to bed, getting ready for school, or going on holiday. When she observed him Martin's playworker was interested to notice that he was most likely to be disruptive on arrival at club just towards the end of club, and before and after snack break. In other words, whenever a change or transition was about to happen.

- Martin's playworker tried to ensure that she always greeted Martin as soon as he arrived. In this way he was made to feel immediately that he had made his presence felt at club. "*Hello, Martin, so glad you're here,*" she used to say so that he had an immediate sense of being welcome.
- Martin was helped to feel valued and to develop an identity at club when he was given responsibility for organising snack time. Having a particular role at club helped to make him feel important and special in his own right.
- Martin's playworkers tried hard to identify his strengths and to provide activities which gave him an opportunity to shine; by experiencing success, he gradually became curious about success!
- Martin's playworker made a point of always saying goodbye to him when he left club and never letting him slip out unnoticed. By doing so, the playworkers were trying to avoid giving Martin an opportunity to feel that it didn't matter to them whether he was in club or not. They also tried to reduce the risk of him feeling in no man's land between club and home by asking him to take something home from club to look after or to prepare or bring in something for an activity the next day. Such requests helped Martin to develop a sense of continuity in his day. In this way a transition became more of a bridge than a vacuum in his mind.

A GOOD WORRY? NOT ALL BAD: UNDERSTANDING WORRIED CHILDREN

An adult can sense when a child is worried about something and this can act as a prompt to take action and then everyone can benefit

"I worry—some people collect stamps, I worry. I'm very good at it."

This playworker's joking pride in her ability to worry is unusual. We do not normally think of worrying as good or acceptable, but rather something that spoils life. Nowhere is this more true than in the life of a child: worried children cause worried, if not distressed, adults; they challenge the myth of childhood as carefree, innocent and playful. They may appear isolated and helpless and are likely to make you, in turn, feel helpless.

"There's something wrong with that child . . . I know there is . . . I just can't get him to talk." We feel worse as we realise that, of course, we can't make children talk about their worries. We know only too well, that if we ask children questions, they give answers—usually the answer they think we want. And it is easy to forget that we are not born able to put our worries into words: we all have to learn to do it. Think of the times you have found it really difficult as an adult to explain the exact nature of your worry to someone else.

Recognising the worried child

The most recognisable worried child is quiet, withdrawn, often pale, and frequently underachieving. But worried children are different from worried adults. Worried adults may feel hopeless; worry in children is often mixed with a persistent hope of recovery. They often believe that their worry can be helped if they can only find the right adult. For this reason, hyperactivity, restlessness, constant attention seeking behaviour can all be an indication that a child is worried and needs an adult to listen. As a nine year old boy said, *"People just don't understand about my feet . . . my feet keep moving 'cos my head is sad."*

Worrying as a solution

"It's no good worrying . . . worrying gets you nowhere."

Maybe there is some truth in this often well-intentioned statement but it flies in the face of child development theory.

Paediatrician and child analyst Donald Winnicott talked of the "nuisance value" of symptoms. Developmentally, children may use worrying as a solution to a problem. Fliss, ten years old, worried her playworkers at holiday club. Timid and anxious, she made little attempt to socialise with other children and stayed close to an adult most of the time. She had prolonged, and sometimes tearful, farewells to her mother in the mornings. As club drew to a close, Fliss hovered anxiously at the front door so her mother was always greeted by a pale and strained little face. After a particularly tearful farewell one day, her playworker said *"You know, you shouldn't make such a fuss, Fliss, don't you know how your mother worries about you?*" She was astonished at Fliss's reply, "*I know mum worries about me. What I don't know is how much.*"

Fliss was using worrying as a solution to her fear that her mother forgot her in the hurly-burly of a busy professional life, that she somehow "fell out" of her mother's mind during the day. What better way to ensure mummy thinks about you than to worry her—the very word implies an exclusive preoccupation. Fliss helps us to understand what worrying is—a kind of work that people need to do! And worrying works: Fliss secured a connection with her mother in that she was worried about Fliss worrying!

Like many children, Fliss had a problem sharing her worries. She was not necessarily being withdrawn or secretive, she simply didn't know how to put such a deep worry into words. And, of course, the paradox was that her main worry was that she didn't want to lose her worry! Her worry was her only way of solving her anxiety, of making sure she had a connection with her mother.

Worrying as a way of looking after someone

Alex, aged twelve, had a different purpose for his worries. His playworker's concern was not that he wouldn't talk about his worries, but shared them endlessly with them and, often late into the night, with his single father. "*I don't mind staying up with him,*" said Alex's dad, "*I like to think I can help.*"

"*Poor old Alex,*" said his playworker one day, "*you're such a worried chap all the time. What would be different if you weren't so worried?*"

Alex thought for a moment. "*My dad might be worried.*"

Alex was using his worries to solve the problem of how he could look after his depressed father. Alex's mother had died very suddenly when he was six years old and his father was still struggling to recover from his loss. He felt inadequate to the task of both mothering and fathering Alex. Alex had learned he could help him to feel he was "a good dad" by supplying him with an endless list of problems for him to solve.

Our worries about worried children

Children's worries worry adults, and this colours our approach to a worried child. Sometimes, children sense their worry may distress an adult. A bereaved eight year old girl asked her mother not to tell her favourite play-worker of her loss "*Cos I don't want Jane to be so sad.*" We can all acknowledge a sense of trepidation, as well as concern, when we approach a worried child. "*You just never know what might be coming.*" said one honest playworker. Yet children's worries can seem so trivial, if not bizarre, to adults. Children going to a new school may often be most worried about whether or not they will be able to find the lavatories. However nonsensical, children need their worries to be taken seriously by adults. When what is real to a child is real to somebody else, then this is what links them to life, the world and meaningful relationships.

How were you worried about?

It might be worth trying to remember what kind of worry were you to your parents. How we manage worried children will also be influenced by how we were managed as children. Hopefully, most of us grew up surrounded by adults who worried about us. Infants and small children have to make adults worry—it is their way of making sure they are held in mind, that someone is thinking about their needs. In this sense, being worried about is reassuring. For older children, being worried about can be restricting! The quality of the way you were worried about and the attitude taken to your childhood worries are the first tools you have to tackle worried children in club. If your childhood worries were taken seriously and calmly, you are likely to be less anxious approaching a worried child than if you were made to feel your childhood worries overwhelmed the adults around you or were ignored or dismissed by them.

Children's worries worry adults and that is to children's credit, and also the essence of what I want to say. Worrying can be a very successful way of a child communicating. You may often sense when a child is worried even if you don't know the exact nature of the worry. This is important because the child will feel their worry has been heard and recognised. Adults may be very preoccupied with the content of a child's worry—"What is the matter?", but for the child, it may be much more important that you simply understand that they are worried. Even children are entitled to a private life—they may choose not to share their worry, but they are reliant on you knowing they are worried.

Talking to worried children

- Ask yourself *"Am I in any way resistant to hearing what this child might have to say?"* Whilst it is natural to feel anxiety when approaching a worried child, we need to be careful that the child does not sense our anxiety and then feel they can't talk to us for fear of upsetting us.

- Avoid direct questions.
- Talk in general terms. For example: "*Some children get worried about . . .*" or "*Boys of ten often worry . . .*"
- Children may relate to "secret feelings" rather than the word "worried". For example: "*Some children may have a lot of secret feelings about . . .*"
- Ask yourself "*What might this worry be a solution to?*"
- Is this child using worrying as a way of not thinking about something?

UNDER PRESSURE: STRESS IN CHILDREN

The word "stress" may be
overused but play leaders do face
an often complex task in helping the
children in their care to cope
with life's pressures

Molly, aged ten, had had a difficult first hour in after school club. Within ten minutes of arriving she had argued with another girl over a packet of sweets which had led to someone pushing someone else causing them to career into the drinks table! Molly's playworker insisted she helped to clear up the mess. Molly felt blamed unfairly and argued over helping with the clearing up, but reluctantly began to swill apple juice round the floor in a dilatory manner. This enraged her playworker, who could see the mess was growing rather than reducing, and there was another flare-up. And so it continued throughout the session, until home time, when the playworkers felt Molly should really be made to "toe the line" and do her share of going home tasks. The more Molly protested the more insistent her playworker became that the tasks were done, until eventually Molly grabbed her coat, spun her on heels and turned at the door to announce, "*Well, thanks for sending me home stressed.*"

We have already thought about how stress is a much overused word nowadays: parents are stressed, employees are stressed, managers are stressed and recently concerns have been expressed at the increasing evidence of some children being stressed. In August 2004, *The Guardian* reported five and a half year olds suffering panic attacks about tests at school (*Guardian*, 2004).

There is no doubt we live in a precarious world and children today are more tested and assessed than children in any previous generation. That said, to talk of children being stressed can be misleading because it suggests that children are like adults and that is not a good move.

Are today's children exposed to any more uncertainty and tension than children raised during World War II, for example, many of whom were separated from their families as evacuees? Those children, of course, were far less influenced by the media, which dictates to today's children not only how they should look but also what they should wear, eat, read and watch on TV and at the cinema. This leads us to believe that today's children are under pressure to succeed in every area of their life.

Complex feelings

The word "stress" originates from the weaving industry— a fabric is stressed when it is pulled too tight. We feel stressed when we feel we are being asked to do more than we are capable of doing, be it physically, emotionally or intellectually.

Molly certainly thought she was "stressed" by her playworker's demands, but was what she was feeling really stress? Irritated, angry, resentful, or fed up may have been more accurate descriptions of how she felt. The risk is that we use "stress" nowadays as a blanket word to cover many experiences, and in play work this really matters because one of our tasks is to help children to understand what they are feeling, to be able to name their feelings and to express their feelings in an appropriate way.

It is a complex task to help children to recognise their feelings because so often they will express them in an inappropriate or immature manner. In club-aged children the symptoms of real stress are likely to be:

- Irritability and aggression.
- Withdrawnness.
- Hyperactivity.
- Loss of appetite.
- Generally feeling low and lacking in energy.
- Thinking and/or talking about running away, truanting and/or harming themselves.
- Finding it hard to talk about worries, feelings or thoughts because they feel "weird".

Flashpoints

What we can be sure about Molly is that she came into club with something on her mind. Stress is accumulative. When we find it difficult to cope we use up energy worrying and so make it more difficult to cope generally. Molly's "flashpoint" was her argument over sweets when she arrived at club. But flashpoints often have very little to do with the child's real stress or worry. Children are as prone to the last straw as adults!

The next evening Molly's playworker discussed her behaviour with her. She asked what sort of day she had had before club. Molly had begun the day angry and resentful because her mother was refusing to let her have her ears pierced like all her friends. Molly knew her mother was adamant about this and there was no point in arguing. On arrival at school she had had an argument with a teacher over a trivial matter and so the day had gone on with Molly arguing with anyone she could. What she needed to stem the flow of arguments was an opportunity to talk about her anger and frustration.

Avoiding stress

There is no doubt that some children suffer stress, and we need to think about situations children of this age may find stressful:

- Argumentative parents.
- Losing touch with a parent or feeling a parent is not interested in them.
- Parental illness.
- Bereavement.
- New baby or step-sibling in the family.
- Beginning secondary school.
- Inconsistency in parental expectations.

Many adults are stressed by such life events, so it is not surprising children react with worry, anxiety and unhappiness. However, the major influence on how children manage such stresses is the behaviour of the adults surrounding them. Adults' stress is contagious and directly linked to the child's level of anxiety. Traumatised children are able to cope and recover when the adults around them give a clear message: "this is painful and difficult but it is manageable and we will help you to manage it." Children's stress is compounded when adults seem unable to cope and, even worse, when a child may feel responsible for looking after a parent during a traumatic life event. We will look at this last area in more depth later in the book, in the chapter "Headline News".

However, it is easy to miss more subtle causes of children's stress: their often frantic attempts to cope with adults' expectations of them. As I said in the Introduction, childcare is more written and talked about now than ever before. Parents seem both more insecure in their parenting and also more concerned about getting it right. Many are filled with an anxiety for their child to be seen to be succeeding. So children are provided with a wide range of extra curricular activities—after school a child is rushed from one activity to another, and then to "crash out" on the computer or in front of the television. Most parents are leading equally frantic lives with full time jobs and employers who seem both more family-friendly and yet more demanding in terms of hours and commitment to the job. It is not unreasonable to suppose that *"hurry up!"* are the most used words in many families before 8.30am!

Parents and children seem to have less time simply to be together. Children have little time to work off the stresses of the day in physical activities such as playing outside freely—additional stress is caused by parents' anxieties about safety when children want to wander off on their own, either on foot or cycling. Parents may feel so anxious about how to parent well that there is a sense of children being unfocussed, with almost too many activities to absorb and not enough time to simply relax and do nothing.

When a child succeeds there is a sense in which it proves that parents have done a good job. And a child's success is a parent's reward for the demanding task of parenting. As a society we now seem to measure success more in academic achievement than in other areas. Practical skills and apprenticeships do not seem to attract the same value, and so it is not surprising that children are under pressure to succeed in school. This pressure comes not only from their parents but also their teachers who are also more assessed and tested than any previous generation of teachers. It is almost impossible for adults not to transmit some of their stresses to the children in their care. And this is also true of playworkers who are now assessed both on their abilities and the provisions available in club.

Molly's playworker was distressed at the end of the week when she was reflecting on what had gone on between her and Molly that evening. "*I know I was sharp with her,*" she said, "*but we knew we had this inspection coming up at the end of the week and I just thought that if Molly behaves like this when they are here . . .*"

She, of course, had no need to feel guilty, for this is a good example of how the pressures of the system place workers under such stress they are prevented from thinking creatively in their work.

How to cope

We should regard stress as a dangerous word. It is a vague word which doesn't help people to understand what they are feeling and how they should manage those feelings. So whenever anyone, child or adult, complains of stress, we need to help them to "unpack", to think a little more broadly and deeply about what is going on for them.

How to manage stress in children

- Help children to identify and name their feelings.
- Encourage children to talk through difficulties rather than just react to them.
- Provide children with opportunities for physical exercise.

Some children do lead stressful lives and find themselves in life situations which cannot be changed or altered. Such children will need help to accept that life for them is difficult but manageable. As one twelve year old said, "*This is my real life . . . it's what's happening now . . . I can't switch channels and watch something else . . .*"

BURSTING INTO TEARS: UNDERSTANDING THE CRYING CHILD

Children who begin to cry at every turn can be very trying, but looking for the real cause of their emotional distress can turn irritation into understanding

No one likes to see a child upset and tearful—indeed, the effect of a child's tears on adults is so strong that we are often moved to comfort and distract the child rather than to stay with their distress and help the child to understand it. The risk in doing so is that children may grow up feeling either that there is something wrong with feeling upset or that distress cannot be thought through and managed, but only soothed away by someone else. However, we all struggle with our feelings when we find ourselves in the position of Cat's playworker. "*I just can't stand that child's whinging and whining,*" she declared. "*She cries over everything, and at the drop of a hat.*" As if on cue, nine year old Cat suddenly let out a wild sob on the other side of the room and rushed over to her playworker, tears pouring down her face. "*Josh pushed me off and he's really hurt my hand,*" she sobbed, holding up a limp but clearly un-damaged hand. "*Oh, for goodness sake, Cat,*" replied her playworker, "*what were you doing to Josh . . .?*"

"*I hate being so tough with Cat,*" she later confided, "*but she can't go through life screaming at the slightest thing.*"

This was a thoroughly human interchange between Cat and her playworker. We can all understand her frustration with a child who seemed to be able to turn tears on and off and who becomes dramatically distressed at the most minor of incidents. Such children can be hard to tolerate. They can make us feel at best irritated and at worst punitive towards them, and so it is important that we try to think about and understand our reactions to them.

Hurt and distress

Children's pain is both raw and evocative for adults. We do not want children to suffer to the extent that we can be sentimental about the innocence and "carefreeness" of childhood. But, of course, children learn to cope with difficulties by experiencing them and by having adults around who help them to negotiate difficulties in a healthy way. So in one sense, an overprotected and struggle-free childhood may be as much a hindrance to having a good life as an adult as a depressed and abusive childhood. One could also argue that it is dangerous to treat children like Cat solely as though they are overreacting. Firstly, this promotes a negative picture of children as being simply manipulative of adults. Secondly, it fails to give meaning to the child's behaviour. We can think of overreacting as a failed communication; it is a child's way of not talking to adults about their troubles because they are anxious about saying exactly what it is that is troubling them. So instead of straight speaking, children like Cat spread their upset all over the place.

Learning to manage our hurt and distress is part of growing up and some children take longer than others.

Sometimes the child who easily resorts to tears is simply immature; they have just not learned more grown up ways of showing they are upset. One nine year old boy stopped mid-tears, open mouthed, when his playworker suggested, "*Quietly, Max, you're too big to make all that noise when you fall over.*" It had simply not occurred to him that there were other ways of coping! What was interesting here was that the staff reported that on occasion Max's mother would turn up at club in tears because her car wouldn't start or she had been delayed at work, incidents which may have frustrated other adults, but which they would have taken in their stride and certainly not been reduced to tears by.

When faced with the "crying child" it is always worth wondering how distress is managed by the adults in the family—maybe Max was offered no other model than crying!

However, Cat's behaviour seemed more indicative of an underlying worry. We began to think of her as a child who had a secret hurt, something she needed to cry about but was too anxious to focus on, and so she cried about everything.

Observing Cat, her playworker noticed that she cried most dramatically at any incident which involved her feeling rejected by other children. When she asked Cat's mother if anything could be worrying her at home, she discovered that Cat had had a series of upsets lately. Her younger sister had outshone her at the swimming gala and her best friend, who lived two doors away, had recently palled up with another girl, leaving Cat in the cold. She had also had a change of teacher, swapping a sympathetic, familiar person for a more formal personality who made no secret of her irritation with Cat's frequent crying.

We began to build a picture of Cat as a child suffering a crisis of self-worth. Her constant crying was attention seeking in the sense we have talked about in previous chapters—she was trying to get close to someone. Cat's secret hurt was that she had become unsure that she was lovable and likeable. Once the club staff were able to think about her in this way, not only was their irritation replaced with sympathy but they were also able to access their own professional skills to manage her appropriately. It goes without saying that the more irritated they were with her, the more un-likeable she felt and the more likely she became to "cry at the drop of a hat."

Fear of rejection

In another club, twelve year old Miles had a different version of the same problem. His playworkers despaired of his hysterical tears whenever he lost a game or was not chosen for an activity. The other children made fun of him as he would sob things like *"It's not fair . . . I never get a chance."* What concerned his playworkers was not only his frequent bursting into tears but also the fact that he seemed unconcerned or affected by the other children's mockery of him. The staff were given a sudden insight into his predicament when in a moment of inspiration, his playworker responded to one of his outbursts about never being given a chance by saying *"So what does that mean, Miles, if you are never given a chance, what does that mean?"* Miles burst out, *"It means no one likes me."*

Miles came from a family of high achievers where success in every area of life was highly valued. Unwittingly, in encouraging Miles to succeed his parents had given Miles the impression that he would be loved *only* if he succeeded. Miles, therefore, construed any minor failure as a threat to his parents' love and approval. At a very deep level, whenever he lost a game or was not chosen for an activity, his unconscious fears of rejection by his parents overwhelmed him. In the same way a bereaved child, or a child who has experienced painful separation, may dissolve into tears frequently, as any pain or upset may remind them of their major loss.

A child crying is a powerful and evocative experience for an adult; the crying child reminds us of our own past and current tears. However, we need to remember that human beings have a repertoire of ways of dealing with emotional distress. Some people get angry, some people close themselves off, some people get stomach-ache, and other people cry easily. Children who cry more than usual have learned somewhere along the line that crying is the best way to cope with distress. Our responsibility as professionals is to help them to discover a choice of appropriate ways of expressing their unhappiness.

Managing the crying child

- Don't ask the child what's wrong—they don't know!
- Don't dismiss frequent tears as an overreaction.
- Do talk to the parents about your concerns.
- Explain to the child that you know they are feeling upset/hurt by the incident that is making them cry but add that you are wondering if anything else is making them feel unhappy at the moment.
- We are right to be concerned about the child who cries too easily but we should be equally concerned, if not

more concerned, about the child who doesn't cry at all. The risk here is that such a child may have given up on the belief that there are sympathetic adults in their world who will listen to their distress.

HEALTHY APPETITES: EATING DISORDERS

How can playworkers manage a child with an eating disorder? How do we recognise the symptoms and help the child to regain control?

That workers in out-of-school clubs should have to think about being aware of eating disorders in children is an interesting reflection on our society. One of the themes in this book is that childhood is changing. As children mature physically at an earlier age, they are becoming increasingly sophisticated in matters of dress and entertainment.

Year 4 and 5 children may be acutely fashion and weight conscious, often filled with a desire to be a Beyoncé or Justin Timberlake look-a-like. In a sense, these children are not being allowed to enjoy their own body shape. What is or is not attractive is being dictated by the media.

And, sadly, we seem to live in a society where appearance is all. Youngsters in Year 6 or 7 are beginning to think about "being fanciable"—and also whom they fancy. Their increasing preoccupation with image and appearance is natural. What we are thinking about in this chapter is an *excessive* or *all-exclusive* worry about weight, or where such a worry is not age-appropriate, as in a seven or eight year old.

What is an eating disorder?

Put simply, an eating disorder is when someone doesn't want to eat, even though there may be no physical cause, such as illness, why they can't eat. The "not wanting to eat" may be mixed with an urge to binge eat followed by vomiting. Eating disorders tend to be associated with girls, but they are becoming an increasing problem in young teenage boys.

What is an eating disorder a solution to?

1—The need for more autonomy

"Make me. Go on, make me eat it . . . you can't, can you?"— twelve year old Jolie challenged her playworker. She attended holiday club every day and it was evident to her playworkers that she was on the brink of developing an eating disorder. Her parents were seeking medical help and had begged the playworkers to make sure that Jolie ate her lunch at club.

Eating disorders are primarily about power and control. As children grow up, they need choices. Even small choices such as what they are going to eat or wear can make a child feel that they have some autonomy in their lives. And choices help us to develop both a sense of identity (I am me and I like eggs) and a sense of privacy.

In the chapter on lying we will be thinking about how young children may feel secure feeling "mummy and daddy know everything about me." The older child needs more sense of a private life. Jolie felt the one thing she could control was what went into her body. And she was right, of course, none of the adults around her could make her eat. We can understand her potential eating disorder as an attempt to gain more independence and control in her own life.

2—The need for less autonomy

By about ten years old, youngsters are beginning to want to explore the world outside home. They are beginning to push boundaries and their sense of exploration is both exciting—and frightening. At times, they are likely to feel on the brink of being out of control, if not actually out of control. Sometimes an eating disorder can be a cry for help. The exact opposite of Jolie, it can be a way of saying "*Please put some boundaries around me and make me feel safe.*"

3—Anxieties about dawning sexuality

"Does puberty hurt?" (nine year old girl.)

"How long is adolescence? I can't hack too much of it." (twelve year old boy)

As they approach puberty children are naturally both excited and anxious about being sexually attractive. They want to be seen as "well fit" but they are also worried about the consequences of being desirable to the opposite sex.

At twelve years old, Georgie was showing no signs of puberty. In contrast to his peers, he had retained his rounded childhood body and chubby cheeks. When he began to lose weight, his after school club workers thought initially that this was the onset of puberty. However, it soon became evident that he was losing excessive weight and was pale and listless as he struggled with the onset of an eating disorder.

Georgie was an only child whose father had died when he was three years old. He and his mother were exceptionally close. What emerged was that Georgie feared adolescence, believing that sexual relationships would separate him from his mother, *"And she'll be all alone then."*

Georgie was terrified of being so overwhelmed by his sexual desires he would abandon his mother completely. He was not eating in an attempt to prevent his body from growing up.

4—Feeling excessive demands to succeed

Eating disorders can arise out of a sense of self-loathing. I have highlighted elsewhere (Clifford-Poston, 2005) that whilst a youngster doesn't have to be competitive and a perfectionist to develop an eating disorder—it helps!

Children have always been under pressure to succeed academically. However, today's children are more tested and graded than any other previous generation. How well a child does or does not achieve academically can be integral to their self-esteem. This is particularly true in homes where education is highly valued and success and achievement may be an ordinary part of family life.

Eleven year old Moira attended a Saturday morning club for gifted children. She was the youngest of three children who had all won scholarships to a prestigious school and had two older siblings who had gone on to Oxford University.

Her club leader had arranged a chess tournament with some other clubs and Moira had reached the semi-final. When she lost her game, she broke down in tears and seemed inconsolable.

Over the coming weeks her play leaders noticed she was not only more quiet and withdrawn, but she was also "binge eating" sweets and biscuits, after which she would disappear to the cloakroom.

How much we consider ourselves to be likeable and loveable, our self esteem, is based on what we feel other people like and value about us.

75

Moira knew her parents valued her "giftedness" and academic success, as indeed they did that of her older sisters. Their well-meaning attempts to praise and encourage her had been misconstrued by Moira. She felt that she was only loveable *if she succeeded*. When she lost the chess game, she felt she had let her family of winners down. She began to think of herself as a loser—not only of the chess game, but of life in general. She began to hate herself.

The most worrying aspect for a youngster at this stage is that self-loathing can very quickly turn into loathing other people. In Moira's case, losing the chess game was equivalent to losing her parents' love.

5—The problem with "good" and "bad" foods

Many youngsters of this age are appropriately self-conscious and health conscious. It is not uncommon for eleven or twelve year olds, particularly girls, to decide to become vegetarian for ethical, political or health reasons. And we live in a world of "good and bad" foods.

Florence's mother had had a major row with the playworkers at after school club. She objected to crisps, sweets and biscuits being sold at club at snack time. She wanted the club leaders to ban these unhealthy foods and replace them with more healthy products such as yoghurt coated raisins.

The play leaders reasoned that labelling foods as "good" or "bad" might cause youngsters to feel guilty or ashamed about what they were eating. It is better to encourage an overall healthy diet, with hopefully only small amounts of junk ('bad') food included. Overly promoting healthy foods can make children rebellious about what they eat!

Of course, both parents and play leaders want to encourage good health in children, but we need to be alert to the risks of being overprotective and anxious about what children eat.

Symptoms of eating disorders

- Sudden and inexplicable loss of weight.
- Refusal to eat or disappearing at meal times.
- Greed and overeating.
- Food faddiness.
- Excessive preoccupation or discussion about body weight.

Managing eating disorders

- If you have concerns that a youngster at club is showing indications of an eating disorder, you must talk to the parents. Eating disorders can be a barometer of the emotional life of a family—they are certainly a barometer of the family's attitude to food. From birth onwards, feeding is a highly emotive issue between parents and children. Nothing worries parents more than a child who cannot or will not eat. Food faddiness can be a child's way of being angry or getting their own back on parents. From a child's point of view, it is always going to make an impact.

- Boost confidence and self-esteem—youngsters like Jolie, Moira and Georgie need to be reminded that most people feel dissatisfied with the way they look. It is best not to argue when they declare themselves

77

unattractive; rather it may be important to give spontaneous, genuine and positive feedback about their appearance at other times, and compliment them on their good qualities of personality.

- Acknowledge that some youngsters may want to eat different foods from the rest of the family or club—vegetarians should be allowed to be vegetarian—and that they may want to break their vegetarian diet on a whim! Allow youngsters as much choice as is feasible, not only over food at club, but also over activities.

IT HURTS:
SELF-HARM

Causing oneself physical
pain and injury is not confined to
depressed teenagers—even some infant
behaviour could be a means to
relieve emotional distress

Why would someone want to hurt themselves deliberately,
often to the extent of needing medical attention? Self-harm
is one of the most puzzling and serious behaviours.

We all consider it normal to avoid pain and seek pleasure. Most of us need to stretch our imagination even to
glimpse the mental state of a self-harmer. And yet self-harm
is a very subtle phenomenon. Lots of things we do or value:
ear-piercing, tattoos, nail biting, body piercing and even
leg waxing, can be a form of self-harm, and yet that doesn't
stop a lot of people from doing them.

Self-harm is most prevalent amongst teenagers, especially
girls, but club workers and teachers are beginning to see
worrying signs in the 8–12 year old age group. All behaviour has meaning and it is worth thinking about how
children develop the idea of self-harm.

Using the body to communicate

As we grow older and more accustomed to the ways of the
world it is easy to lose track of how unfamiliar and strange
the world may seem to a small child. So much of life is
familiar to us as adults that we can forget how vulnerable

in the world children may feel. The only world very young children know and are intimate with is the world of their parents. Indeed, very young children's knowledge is confined to that of their own bodies and their parents' bodies.

Small children are preoccupied with bodies; what goes into them, what comes out of them, how they work and what they can do with them. Unusual bodily conditions such as diarrhoea can be overwhelming and terrifying for them, as such an experience may feel like a sudden assault on their familiar world. So it is not surprising that children use their bodies as one of their first means of communicating with adults.

A hungry or tired baby has no other way of expressing their needs to their mother than by crying, wriggling, kicking, turning red in the face, using their whole body to communicate. The role of a "good enough" parent is to make sense of these bodily expressions and, as the child grows, help them to both find names for their needs and feelings and to express them verbally.

However, even as adults we will rely on our bodies to communicate what we can't put into words; for example: banging our fists in rage or squirming with disgust. This is so acceptable that it has even crept into child care.

For example, one of the risks of encouraging angry children to hit a cushion to get rid of their rage is that it perpetuates both the idea that strong feelings can only be expressed physically and that angry feelings are not an appropriate part of relationships.

Babies

Babies are soothed by rhythmical body movements. We comfort them instinctively by rocking, patting and walking with them. Babies soon devise ways to recreate this comfort for themselves using harmless rhythmic comfort habits such as stroking themselves or using a "cuddly."

But if a baby feels very stressed, angry or frustrated, they may resort to more serious actions such as banging their head on the side of the cot, seemingly causing themselves pain on purpose. Many babies will head bang occasionally, particularly if they are trying to get to sleep, but persistent or violent head banging is a serious communication.

Two to five year olds

It is not uncommon for nursery staff to express concern that a toddler has the *habit* of, for example, nail biting or head banging. We need to be careful here: we all have our own idiosyncratic ways of expressing ourselves; some are more acceptable than others.

Some toddlers may develop head banging as their "thing" when they feel anxious and troubled, just as others may wet the bed. (*"You mean head banging is his equivalent of my eating chocolate?"* declared one nursery nurse worried about her two year old charge!) We need to observe carefully when a child has a self-harm habit. When does it happen? Is there any pattern? For example, does he always head bang just as his mother leaves, or even just as she arrives? Our main concern should be when a toddler is using self-harm as their only and automatic way of communicating distress. What the child is doing then is trying to rid their body of a pain which seems unbearable, for example the pain of feeling abandoned as mother leaves.

If they are not comforted by the movement of their body they may resort to seeking their own pain. Psychologically, the reasoning is that a self inflicted pain may seem preferable to one that you cannot control.

Five to eight year olds

As children begin to grow up they have to reconcile the person they are with the person their parents want them to be! In the early years children's main aim is to please their parents but gradually it becomes more important to them to do and be what *they* want to be. This is a risky process as unconsciously the child may be afraid that they will lose their parents' love. It takes a lot of courage for a child not to want to please their parents.

When parents do not understand this conflict the child may feel they need to be punished, either for what they feel they have done or for what they want to do. Children may punish themselves by "attacking" their bodies through something like nail biting, hair pulling, picking at their skin, etc. They may also seek physical comfort from the pain of worry through masturbation. And of course, such a child is in a huge internal muddle; they are not only fearful but also angry and frustrated.

Small children live in a world of "magic thinking" where just to think something can make it happen! It is normal for children to wish their parents dead, or at least exiled for a while! At the same time, of course, they do not want this to happen.

When a child feels it is not safe to express their aggression they may redirect it from the outside world onto themselves. It can feel safer to do something bad to yourself than to wish something bad on the adults who care for you. For who will care for you if those adults disappear?

Eight-plus years

There is no evidence that the toddler who rocks or the five year old who head bangs necessarily goes on to develop the most serious forms of self-harm, such as cutting and slashing the body. Self-harm in the betweenage and teen stage tends to be dramatic and lurid. It raises the questions, "What are the child's parents like?" and "what does the child have to do to feel they have made an impact on their parents?"

Self-harm is one of the most intimately violent things a child can do to their parents. They are attacking their own body rather than attacking their parents and it is the most powerful way a child can communicate with a parent. Such a child is in a serious muddle. Just as younger children inflict pain to rid their bodies of pain, so an older child may also inflict pain in order to seek comfort from the wound. We can think of this as them giving themselves permission to have a plaster, a bandage, etc. The wound means that someone has to tend to them even if it is only themselves. Plasters and bandages are, of course, all symbols of TLC. So what we have is a very distressed youngster seeking pain as a form of pleasure.

Self-harm is genuinely mysterious and we may have to accept that it is something we can never understand fully. The teen who self-harms has decided that pain is pleasurable and we have to accept that for such a youngster self-harm is addictive because the pain is so pleasurable.

That said, many people will admit to feeling most alive when they are angry and none of us can forget that we know intensely that we are alive when we are in great pain.

A depressed and unhappy teenager may self-harm as a way of reminding themself that they are alive, they are not as dead as they feel. As one tween said, "*When I cut myself and the blood comes out, I know I'm not a nobody.*"

PART THREE:
JUST ATTENTION SEEKING?

HELLO, I'M HERE!
THE BOISTEROUS AND
SHOWING-OFF CHILD

Sometimes boisterousness
and showing off can be a child's way
of telling you they are afraid of not
being noticed and heard

The staff of a holiday club were discussing new arrivals. Several commented on ten year old Josh. *"He's such a boisterous child, quite a problem,"* said one, *"You have to watch Josh all the time."* As she finished speaking another playworker entered the room, and hearing Josh's name, said *"Josh? He's such a lively child, isn't he? Curious about everything..."*

As I said in the Introduction, "problem behaviour" is very much a matter of how a child's behaviour is construed. We seem to live in a society obsessed with labelling children, and labels range from the benign ('show off', for example) to medical labels such as "ADHD". So what might prompt an adult to feel they have to label a child?

"Well, it's nice to put a name to a problem... makes you feel you can do something about it..." said one playworker. And it is true, a label helps us to feel we have a clear picture of the problem and, therefore, guidance and help in managing the child. But, of course, this is not necessarily true. Indeed, we risk presuming things may be so for a child when they are not because that is how it is for all children with that label! In doing so, we risk missing the unique "particular" for each child. Perhaps we really label as a way

of coping with two feelings. Firstly, when a child has a problem our unconscious fear is that an adult has not done something they should. So we can think labelling not only makes adults feel more competent, it also blames the child! Secondly, children's dependency is a huge responsibility for adults. Child care is worrying enough when we feel we understand the child and know how to manage them. When we feel we don't understand and don't know what to do, it can be hard to tolerate the sense of uncertainty and "not knowingness." Labelling the child can sometimes fool us into thinking we do know and understand. So as we think in this article about the boisterous and showing-off child, we need to bear in mind that there are probably as many reasons for boisterousness and showing off as there are children.

The boisterous child

It is interesting how affectionately we can talk of a boisterous toddler. The toddler's struggle to establish who they are and to master new skills is endearing (if exhausting!). Boisterousness in club age children, however, can be very irritating to both adults and other children. We expect this age group to be much more competent and more sure of who they are, and so how do we understand children like Josh? And how does a boisterous child differ from a lively child? These playworkers were in no doubt about the distinction: a lively child is likely to be full of fun and curiosity, but also able to control and contain their exuberance. A boisterous child like Josh, on the other hand, seemed unable to help overdoing his exuberance for life. *"He's so in the other kids' faces, they can't handle it,"* commented his key worker

Josh was the eldest of four children close together in age. Both parents worked long hours and his mother volunteered that Josh took on more responsibility for his siblings than was appropriate for a child of his age. As he helped to care for the younger children in the family he was left feeling that to get this own needs met he had to make them known twice as loudly as the others. We began to think about his boisterousness in club as his way of ensuring that he was heard, emotionally as well as physically, by other people. He did not seem able to trust the adults around him to notice him and meet his needs unless he was over-demanding by being loud.

We also thought about Josh's behaviour as an extreme of ordinary developmental behaviour for this age group. They are in the process of looking forward to adolescence and becoming more sexual. They are a little more independent of their parents and have the freedom to act things out more. On the whole, life may feel a little more dangerous or, as Josh described, "*It's more fun, but a bit more scary.*" Boisterousness can sometimes be a way of making sure the adults keep an eye on you whilst you are moving slowly away from the safety of your parents' care. It is, if you like, a way of saying "*Don't forget about me as I move out of sight.*" As we heard at the beginning, Josh made at least one playworker feel that she had to watch him all the time. Sometimes betweenagers will behave in an exaggerated way to show the adults that they feel a bit unsafe and at risk.

Showing off

In a different club, Lucy, at the same age, was a worry to her play staff. She was a lively, attractive and capable girl who just could not help showing off. As well as her more general, silly and over-the-top behaviour, the staff had noticed how she would raise her voice as playworkers passed her group as though desperately wanting the adult to pay attention to her. The staff were divided in their understanding of her; some felt she needed to be ". . . *slapped into place. She's just attention seeking.*" Others felt this was extreme behaviour for a girl her age and indicative of serious underlying problems.

We have been thinking about how it is interesting that almost any adult describing a child as "attention seeking" does so in a negative and dismissive way by invariably adding, "just". It is as though there is both something wrong with having needs and trying to get those needs met, and also that attention seeking behaviour does not have to be taken seriously or need a response. The child who shows off for attention is trying to get close to someone but, sadly, their difficult behaviour is more likely to irritate and anger adults than to elicit warmth and affection. When we think of attention seeking as attachment seeking, we find it easier to manage.

Lucy's mother had suffered from severe post-natal depression for the first three years of Lucy's life. They had never managed to bond successfully and Lucy had the feeling that she was left dangling, and was desperately trying to attach to an adult. Boisterous behaviour, showing off, and hyperactivity are often a child's way of communicating that they do not feel secure, grounded and contained in their relationships with the adults around them; I am not suggesting that conditions such as ADHD are *only* a failure to attach, but it may be a significant element for some children.

Lucy had another reason for her dramatic and exaggerated behaviour. Children living with depressed parents often feel they have to work very hard to make an impact on their parents. Just as Josh felt he was only heard when he was loud, Lucy felt she had to be the life in the family. By this I mean she felt she had to bring her mother to life by being very lively herself. By being a "larger than life" personality she was trying to both elicit a lively response from her depressed mother, and also to cheer her up. Showing off can be a child's way of being the family anti-depressant.

What is it about the showing off child that worries adults? It is, of course, one area that highlights the disparity between adults and children. Children show off naturally; adults have to do it in a culturally acceptable form such as through the arts or entertainment. When showing off in a boisterous, silly way children are using their bodies to invite us to share excitement. They are not only saying "*Look at me,*" they are also saying "*I want to be looked at.*" Such excess of vitality can remind adults of how showing off, with all its links to sex, has become a problem for them. And that is interesting, because if no two people ever showed off to each other, then no couples would ever get together!

As we thought about Lucy, one of her playworkers recounted a story of taking a group of younger children to a park. As they ran into the play area one girl, followed by several others, began to turn cartwheels over the grass. "*I longed to join in,*" said the playworker, "*but I knew those days were over and I felt really sad.*" We began to wonder if showing off is also a problem to adults because it reminds us of a more lively, unrestrained and carefree time of our lives we have learnt to repress and so lose.

Managing boisterousness and showing off

- The risk of saying "*Don't show off,*" for example, is that it may make the child feel more distant from you and doesn't give them a more appropriate way of expressing their needs.

- Make the child feel you are aware of them in club by always greeting them when they arrive and talking to them throughout the session. Comments like, *"Are you enjoying that, Lucy?"* will enhance the feeling that you have your eye on them.

- Offer the child a more appropriate way of expressing their needs by explaining to them that they may be worried you won't hear them unless they are boisterous and noisy but actually noisiness sometimes prevents people from listening rather than helping them to listen more!

WINNING AND LOSING: COPING WITH COMPETITION

Playworkers need to realise when a child's reaction means they are struggling to deal with either success or failure

Nine year old Jason was regarded as a sensitive child who found it difficult to join in at club. Everyone was delighted when he eventually made a best friend in Toby. He became more cheerful and outgoing and seemed to be enjoying club.

But suddenly there was a problem: Jason decided he didn't want to go to club any more, explaining he didn't want to "do badges". This was a new activity where the children were given badges on completion of various tasks, such as learning to cook. His playworkers and parents were worried and disappointed. "*He seemed so much more confident, we thought he'd be delighted to have a go with Toby,*" said his parents. They thought that Jason was "*afraid to try . . . he's afraid of failing in front of Toby.*" His playworker agreed, adding "*Yes, not at all like Jock,*" and she pursed her lips and frowned slightly, "*he just has to win . . . you just can't hold him back.*"

Children have to learn to cope with both success and failure. We tend to focus on the pleasures of success; children may have to be reminded not to gloat or boast, but on the whole adults are likely to worry more about helping children with failure.

Jason's playworker was sympathetic and concerned about him; she found it hard to conceal her irritation with Jock. In their urgent and constant struggle for success, competitive children remind us of how we feel about our desire to do better or have more than other people. This worries us because we know that competition and aggression go hand in hand.

Winning often demands a certain ruthlessness, we talk of "stepping over the bodies on the way up," meaning someone has been single minded in their pursuit of success, aggressively disregarding the needs of others.

In a sense, there is nothing inherently wrong with aggression; the problems with aggression lie in how it is expressed. Children need to be taught how to be aggressive and competitive in an appropriate way. Adults also need to understand what a complicated experience both winning and losing is for children (and for adults too!).

Learning to compete

Our first experience of competition is in the family. There is only one mother and one father, both of whom have limited resources. Children have to compete, consciously or unconsciously, for their parents' attention, from both other siblings, and the parents as a couple.

We often presume that only children do not suffer from sibling rivalry but they do, of course, in the sense that all children fear that their parents would rather be with each other than with them. In families, we call this competition envy and jealousy, qualities which are usually discouraged or criticised.

Envy and jealousy are part of everyday family life and we need to understand the difference. Envy occurs between two people when one person wants to spoil something for the other. For example, we are all familiar with the child who spoils their sibling's birthday party with their truculent and difficult behaviour. Jealousy occurs between three or more people with the jealous person trying to take something from someone else, For instance, it is not uncommon for a brother to steal his sibling's girlfriend!

So competition is about aggression, about fighting for what we feel we want and need, but it is also about guilt. Competition in the family may make children feel in a double bind: if they triumph they may feel guilty and ashamed because they are afraid they may have robbed, outdone or even harmed someone else in the family. If they fail they risk feeling unworthy and unloved and, as we thought about earlier on, children take these personal and family experiences into the wider world of school and club, where there are so many more people in the competition.

Fear of failure or fear of success?

Let's think again about Jason, who was clearly frightened and worried about doing badges. Both his parents and playworkers had tried to encourage him to have a go, assuring him, "*It doesn't matter if you don't win a badge.*" Eventually his playworker said "*Jason, you mustn't worry about not winning a badge.*"

"*I'm not,*" said Jason. His playworker laughed and said, "*Well, you mustn't worry about winning a badge either,*" and then seeing the expression on Jason's face, she asked gently, "*What might be worrying about winning a badge?*"

Jason paused and thought before saying hesitantly, "*Well, Toby might not get one . . .*"

This was the key to Jason's fear of success. Jason was afraid to try in case he succeeded! He was worried that Toby wouldn't like him any more if he won a badge and Toby didn't, but he was also worried that if he *won* a badge that would be the reason why Toby might *fail* to win one.

Such children experience success as a cake—if they get a slice then there is automatically less for everyone else. Jason didn't want to outstrip Toby and he also didn't want Toby to envy him.

His parents also recalled how Jason had come home proudly from holiday club one day with a model he had made. Later they overheard Toby commenting that as he hadn't been at club that day, he hadn't got a model. Jason immediately destroyed his model, saying "*There, I haven't got one now, we're the same.*" We might not like feeling envious and jealous but it can be even more worrying to feel envied, to feel you have more than someone else.

Jason had been bullied by Joanne, his resentful older sister. When Jason was two, his sister's adored Godmother gave him a present. Joanne burst into tears, sobbing "*Oh no, she's with him now, she loves him now . . . she doesn't want me.*" Jason had learned in the family that the consequence of being envied was that you might be attacked. We began to understand his reluctance to try was his way of trying to look after himself.

The pleasures of failing

Psychologically, there are advantages in failing or not trying. Jason was being successful in concealing his shame and guilt about feeling competitive. If he didn't win a badge, he may have felt ashamed that he had let himself down or guilty that he had let other people down. By failing to join the competition, Jason was both avoiding exposure and gaining the sympathetic support of the adults.

Being successful is directly linked to growing up and being independent. Psychotherapist Adam Phillips has highlighted how some children who are afraid to try are asking the question, *"If I succeed, who will look after me?"* Their lack of confidence lies in their anxiety as to whether or not they can lead a successful life without their parents to look after them. By failing or not trying, they are literally avoiding the test and trying to buy more time in childhood.

The child who has to win

Let us return to Jock, who was always first to volunteer, first to have a go, energetic and full of enthusiasm; he would throw himself at any task or activity—until he thought he was losing, when he would become angry and frustrated and walk away protesting, *"It's not fair . . . I was winning."*

Describing someone as competitive is often critical or derisory, as though there is something wrong with wanting to succeed. There is nothing wrong with being competitive as such, but the problem for children like Jock is they confuse being "the best" and being "the best Jock."

Jock was the youngest of five children by eight years. As he grew up his siblings always seemed stronger, wiser and cleverer than him. He couldn't compete with them and win, and so he thought he could never be "the best". And because his siblings seemed to have so many more privileges than him he feared he would only be loved and valued if he was better than everyone else. He felt under pressure to prove his place in the world, and was worried that only the winners get noticed. He was trapped in a vicious circle. He felt unsure he was loved and valued: he strove to win to gain validation; he then felt aggressive and disliked for his behaviour; he then strove to win, and so on.

So the over-competitive child is often more insecure and worried than the child who refuses to try. We could say that the child who refuses to try believes deep down inside them that they might succeed. Children like Jock feel they have to prove they can succeed and their self-esteem is very fragile. If they win they feel temporarily loveable and if they lose their self-worth plummets.

Managing the under- and over-competitive

Jason and Jock shared the same problem: they were both insecure about how they felt about themselves. The child who will not try needs to be encouraged to think about their worries over winning and triumphing. After all, there is nothing wrong with being triumphant, is there? The over competitive child needs help to think about their anxieties in failing.

"I'M BORED":
UNDERSTANDING THE
LAZY CHILD

When children seem lazy and unmotivated they may be trying to avoid painful issues

We are born curious—as anyone who has ever watched a baby will know. Even very young babies observe, push and pull their own world in an often furious attempt to learn about it. And well into their first year mothers will declare, with a mixture of pride and exhaustion, "*Oh, he's into everything now.*" So in this sense, a lazy child is a contradiction in terms. And yet it is a relatively common experience for playworkers to have to cope with a child who seems unmotivated and disinterested.

Eleven year old Penny was just such a child. She was a rather plump girl, an only child, who had been attending after school club for nearly a year. Her playworkers had become increasingly irritated by her. "*She just won't make an effort,*" said one. "*She just seems bland about whatever we offer her.*" Another volunteered "*She never does more than the necessary. If you ask her to help clear up she will, but she never just kicks in and helps. It's the same with activities: if we didn't chivvy her along she'd just sit there like a huge steam pudding.*"

Lazy children can make adults feel angry. They remind us of that indolent aspect of ourselves, which we would rather forget; the aspect of us that would just like to sit about and be waited upon. That is human! However, we do need to take the lazy child seriously. First and foremost, a tired child, lacking in vitality, needs to see a doctor. Lethargy in children is often a symptom of an underlying physical illness. When illness is ruled out, we need to understand children's laziness as a communication. Let's think about Penny.

Laziness as a protest

Penny's playworkers were presuming from Penny's demeanour that she was probably a somewhat doted on and indulged child. In fact, her arrival had been unplanned and interrupted her busy parents' career plans. Whilst there was no doubt they loved her, her mother admitted, "*We decided from the word go that she would have to fit in with us, she wasn't going to change our lives.*" So Penny had always had a very strict routine which provided her with very few choices. As a small child she was compliant but as she reached the later years of childhood she felt more and more constrained and restricted. Family life was lived at a pace and Penny soon began to realise non-compliance, i.e., laziness, gave her a sense of independence and freedom. "*The more busy my mum is, the slower I get, and she can't do anything about it,*" she said laughingly. Of course, protests can become a way of living. Penny was using laziness in club as a way of warning the adults: "*Don't try and organise every minute for me.*" She feared that if she responded enthusiastically to her playworkers they would take her over and, ironically, her laziness produced just that result. Irritated by her lack of effort, her playworkers would try to pressurise her into taking a more full part in club. They had to change their approach by offering her as much choice as possible and by also sometimes allowing her to be just lazy.

Laziness as a way of not feeling

Eight year old Peter was always bored and tired at holiday club. He would arrive yawning, frowning and turning up his nose at whatever was on offer. "*It's boring,*" he would say. His playworkers were concerned. "*He just doesn't seem to want to do anything . . . it's not right in a boy of this age.*" They decided to talk to his mother and find out what he was like at home. "*He's always been the same,*" she said. "*I'm afraid he's just sullen.*" Undeterred, Peter's playworker pursued his history with his mother. She was soon able to pinpoint a change in Peter's behaviour about a year after his father had left when he was five. He and his father had been close and initially his father had visited Peter regularly. Then he took a job further away and contact gradually ceased. Peter's mother explained that Peter used to ask about his father a great deal "*but he used to get so upset I suggested we didn't talk about him any more*"

In discussing Peter we wondered how he was coping now with his feelings about his father. Not talking about feelings which upset us doesn't necessarily help us to stop experiencing them. We wondered if being bored was a retreat for Peter in the sense that boredom is a feeling without feelings: just blandness and numbness.

The next time Peter said he was bored, his playworker asked him "*If you weren't feeling bored now, what would you be feeling?*" There was a pause before Peter's eyes filled with tears. "*I'd be sad and mad . . . 'cos of my dad,*" he said.

Lazy children may actually be busily working hard! They are hard at work not to feel something painful and difficult which they feel they cannot share with the adults around them. It is always worth thinking of "laziness" as a cover for another feeling.

The fear of finding out

In spite of the difference in their ages, Penny and Peter shared a fear. Penny's playworkers were able to talk to her teachers and discovered her attainments were well behind both her chronological age and her ability. Her teachers also described her as lazy: "*She's bright enough, she just won't do the work.*"

In order to learn, children need to feel free to be curious, to let their minds roam. If they feel there is a secret, something it would be bad to find out about, then they censor their curiosity. Peter didn't understand why his father had left and was afraid to find out in case, as he dreaded, it was his fault. Deep inside herself, Penny feared that she may not have been wanted by her parents. She knew instinctively they were resentful as well as delighted about her birth. She couldn't ask why and so was afraid to let her curiosity roam in case she made an unwelcome discovery. Such children may choose to struggle not to learn about much at all rather than risk learning about something which feels forbidden or painful.

Sometimes children need to be lazy

We have already thought about how parents today seem under real pressure to prove their successful parenting, and sometimes it seems as though there is a mythical equation between the number of out-of-school activities a child takes on and the quality of their parenting! Very few children can now roam freely after school. Some simply watch television or videos/DVDs, but many from a very early age have a full diary of activities each evening. Whilst in many ways this may enhance both a child's development and education, the drawback is that relaxation is a serious and necessary business. We need laziness to recover from the hurly-burly of daily life, and laziness is a natural process of recuperation and renewal. "Rolling all over the floor doing nothing" is an integral part of a child's development. And this is particularly important for club aged children, who may seem at times to do nothing but lie immobile on their beds for hours at a time conserving energy whilst listening to music so loud that the very foundations of the house seem to shake. At other times, there seems to be a suspicious silence emitting from the bedroom. But being a between-ager is hard work and they may not in fact be "wasting time". They may not be meditating upon the finer points of the great philosophical thinkers, but they are practising being independent in many ways. Most important is their need to *"feel whatever I want to feel,"* as one twelve year old described it, to have time and space to find meaning for their welter of new feelings and experiences (Clifford-Poston, 2005). And club, which provides a transitional space between home and school, may provide betweenagers with a crucial time to absorb and process life.

Finally, some children are more contemplative than others and we need to remember this when taking the lazy child seriously. Such children may need more time and space to process the hum of their curiosity. At this age, children's heads are buzzing with all sorts of thoughts and ideas which need to be processed and digested. So perhaps an important question for club workers to ask themselves is, *"How much time are we setting aside for children to be lazy in club?"*

SERIOUSLY FUNNY? UNDERSTANDING THE CLUB CLOWN

Children may take on the role of clown in club as a defence mechanism to hide their anxieties. Here are some suggestions of ways for playworkers to understand what lies behind the laughter

Eleven year old Tim was worrying his playworkers; clumsy and overweight, he was regarded by his class mates as "weird". He had no special friends and tended to always be on the fringe of any group. The first week of holiday club had followed a predictable pattern, with the other children shrugging him off.

Then came the day of a trip to an adventure club, where the children could take turns on a small assault course. The group watched as Tim took his turn to try to balance across a rope ladder stretched between two walls. Suddenly he fell spectacularly, arms and legs waving and rolling along the mat as he landed. The other children laughed and clapped. *"Oh, go on Tim, do it again!" one said,* and Tim, initially embarrassed, suddenly beamed and bowed.

Over the next week Tim's playworkers noticed that he was now taking every opportunity to act the club clown, making a fool of himself in order to amuse the others. He was also keeping up a barrage of silly jokes. Moving far too close to another child he would giggle enthusiastically *"Have you heard this one?"*

His playworkers noticed these jokes were coming thick and fast all day and for some reason it was making them anxious. *"He just tries too hard,"* said his key worker, who had tried to encourage Tim to ease off the joke telling, *"it puts the other kids off."*

Tim seemed genuinely surprised at her comments. He tried to persuade her that the other children liked his clowning because they laughed; what he was missing was that his peers were increasingly laughing at, rather than with, him. Sometimes, they were clearly embarrassed by the silliness of his behaviour.

Clowning as a communication

In order to understand the club clown we need to think about humour and jokes in general. All humour contains an element of surprise. We are never quite sure how a joke is going to end or exactly what a clown may do next.

On the whole, children find surprises exciting and fun. Adults often feel a vague sense of unease around a surprise. When playworker Pip was leaving club after three years, both the children and staff wanted to give him a surprise party. Although touched and overwhelmed, he seemed somewhat uneasy about the whole event. Later, he explained: *"Well, it was a lovely thing to do, and I really appreciated it, but I felt cast in their plot."* He had been feeling sad about leaving club but felt he had to behave in an expected, delighted way.

As adults, we may feel slightly anxious around children's jokes and humour because humour also carries this sense of being cast in the teller's plot. There is a prescribed response: we are expected to laugh, and we can really suffer on a child's behalf when we can anticipate that their joke is simply not going to be funny.

Young children's humour is relatively easy to manage because it tends to be tried and tested, and predictable: *"What did the biscuit say when it got run over?"* Answer: *"Crumbs!"* Everyone knows more or less what's coming, everyone knows how to respond.

Small children acting the clown are relatively easy to manage. They tend to mimic adults and re-enact behaviour they have witnessed. This clowning may give unwanted or embarrassing revelations about family life, but the innocent nature of small children's humour usually makes it manageable. The older child who plays the clown can be more worrying for us.

Freud argued that we use jokes and humour to help us deal with our unacceptable feelings. Tim was worried about making friends. He felt he had found a solution accidentally to his poor social skills at the activity centre. The problem was that while this incident could have been an excellent ice-breaker for his peer relationships, Tim had come to see it as his only way of being accepted by his peers.

The risk of being a clown is that while you may feel people like you, it is difficult for people to take you seriously. Tim still had the problem of having no real friends: he was still never chosen to be in anyone's team, for example.

Clowning and aggression

Freud also said that the essence of jokes lies in the truth it contains. There are times when we all use humour to say something we felt unable to deal with directly. The club clown can be a disturbing influence in this way.

Sylvia, aged eleven, had a very ready wit and could quickly hone in on other children's Achilles heel. She could be relied upon to bestow a clever nickname or impersonation. The other children found her amusing and fun but they were also cautious about her, realising the cruelty in her humour. One incident brought the matter to a head for the club staff. A new girl arrived in club, somewhat brighter and more attractive than Sylvia. Her name was Sasha, known as Sash, and Sylvia quickly nicknamed her "Trash". Sasha would smile weakly but was clearly uncomfortable with this ridiculing of her name.

Freud pointed out that we never really know what we are laughing at. In slapstick humour, such as someone slipping on a banana skin, we laugh because the person looks amusing with arms and legs flying in the air. We laugh at the same time as being aware that for the person this is really not very funny. Freud argues that we are also laughing out of relief that it is not us who has fallen over.

We came to understand Tim and Sylvia as working hard for their peers by being the club clown. The other children felt secure in the fact that while everyone was laughing at Tim and Sylvia no one would be laughing at them.

Children in Years 9 and 10 may be experiencing tidal waves of strong emotion, including aggression and sexual desire. These two feelings are closely linked and children of this age may be afraid of being overwhelmed by both. They are prone to use humour as a way of showing aggression. They want to be popular, to be in with the group. Nothing makes one feel more in with the group than when people laugh at one's jokes. So by expressing aggression through humour, Sylvia and Tim felt they could remain attractive people within the group because if the joke fell flat, for example by Sasha feeling hurt, they could

107

always react with something like: *"But I was only joking,"* or *"Can't you take a joke?"*

Clowning and anxiety

Clowning can also be a way children of this age deal with fears about themselves. Sasha had a lively and attractive manner and had quickly become the focus of the girl groups. It was clear to Sylvia's club workers that she felt threatened by Sasha. They were as concerned about Sylvia as they were about protecting Sasha from Sylvia's unkind humour. They felt that Sylvia was trying to use humour to hint to them that she now felt she was at risk of being the "trash" in the group.

Clowning and boredom

As I was putting the finishing touches to this chapter I discussed its main points with a club worker. After expressing a degree of interest in what I had to say, she suddenly shrugged her shoulders and said *"Of course, once they start clowning about, they are often bored."* This is certainly an important point to hold in mind, especially if you find more than one child in club clowning continuously or persistently.

Managing the club clown

Sylvia and Tim had come to believe their identity in the group was dependant upon them being funny. We have to help children to understand that there is a difference between using humour to cope with a difficult experience (adults do it all the time) and to avoid acknowledging difficulties in an experience. This does not mean that they have to lose their humorous ways but only that they should not feel solely dependant upon them.

- We need to be extremely sensitive in our management of such children. It can be so easy to be a killjoy, which can be crushing for the child. Our main aim has to be to ensure that a child is not stuck in the role of club clown. Other children in club can be funny and the club clown can be serious.
- It goes without saying that the club clown should never be confronted about their behaviour in public.
- Perhaps the best way to manage the club clown is to talk to them privately, with or without their parents, along the lines that you have sensed that when they are feeling anxious or unhappy they feel they have to be funny.

PART FOUR:
WORRYING BEHAVIOUR

WON'T PLAY, CAN'T PLAY: UNDERSTANDING ANTISOCIAL CHILDREN

So many children socialise easily that we presume it is instinctive, forgetting that they have to learn how to do it

What an extraordinary transition it is from being someone special in the family to being one of many in a group! Making friends is as much a developmental stage as learning to walk and talk. Children master skills in their own time and at their own pace. Some will always be more content with their own company—there is nothing wrong with that—but by eight years old most will have made some form of friendship, so the child who is unable to relate easily to other children needs to be taken seriously. Enjoying your own company is different from being isolated.

The shy child

Children are not born shy—some are born more sensitive and vulnerable than others, some more extrovert than others—but shyness is not a personality trait; it is a learned solution to anxiety provoked by the fear of not being liked.

Children begin to learn to get on with others in the family. Peer relationships will mirror family relationships. Very authoritarian parents or parents who make too high or rigid demands can make a child fear "getting it wrong," in other words, making mummy or daddy angry. The child then approaches other children with the same anxiety. Inconsistent parenting can have the same effect—a child may become tentative because they never know if they have "got it right."

Shyness can also be a solution to another problem. Nine year old Lucy, the youngest of five, was frequently bossed around by her older siblings. She grew up both anxious to please them, and angry with them. She approached other children unconsciously afraid she would attack them. Shyness can be a way of saying *"Look, I'm not angry or a threat to anyone."*

Managing shy children

- Shyness can become a habit. Help the shy child to practice being with people in other ways than being shy.
- Be sympathetic but not over-concerned. Over-concerned adults may reinforce shyness by anticipating that the child will be anxious in any new situation.
- Avoid persuading the shy child to join in. Gently offer invitations, clearly explaining exactly what the activity is about and what the child will be expected to do, so reducing their anxiety about "not knowing".
- Provide activities where the child can join in both as an observer and a participant.
- Encourage "Buddy" systems, which can be very useful.
- Introduce the shy child to activities in pairs or small groups.
- Reassure them that it doesn't matter whether they get it right or wrong. Warm, gentle praise helps them to feel they are loved and accepted for themselves.

The withdrawn child

Mark was pale, sad and sometimes agitated. He would often sit with his back to other children or wander off to find a space for himself. When encouraged into the group, he sat silently, seemingly to be in a world of his own.

Withdrawn children can go unnoticed because their behaviour is not disruptive. The less formal atmosphere of the after school club had enabled Mark's playworker to notice his lack of friends immediately. Withdrawn behaviour is not just a social problem, it is a real communication from the child that the world is troubling them. *"At school, sometimes I cry in my head,"* said Mark. When the real world is frightening, a child may retreat into a dream world. Everyone daydreams, but the withdrawn child is rarely "awake".

Managing withdrawn children

- Remind withdrawn children you are aware of them even though they seem unaware of you. Make a point of greeting them on arrival. Mark's playworker tried to check on him every fifteen minutes or so by calling out, *"OK, Mark?"*
- Talk to the child's parents to see if there is anything particular worrying the child.
- Remember that withdrawn children are in a serious muddle and may sometimes need specialist help.

The aggressive child

Aggressive children are the most difficult group of children to manage in after school club. They frighten and repel other children. They can frighten adults—because they make us want to be aggressive in return.

To get on with other people we have to learn to cope with conflict. Most friendships have their difficulties and disagreements. A risk of promoting playing nicely is that it suggests that there is only one way of socialising. Conflict is part of socialising. However, there is a big difference between a child being aggressive and a child only being aggressive.

Aggression is a solution to feeling powerless and vulnerable. You know how much stronger you feel when you are angry than when you are sad. Aggressive children are trying to take control and almost bully people into being their friends. They then get into a vicious circle: afraid they won't be liked, they try to bully other children into liking them but behave in a way that ensures they are not liked! However, we can be much more optimistic about the aggressive child than the withdrawn child. The aggressive child is trying to get close to other children in an inappropriate way, the withdrawn child may already have given up.

Managing aggressive children

- The more an aggressive child is ignored, the more aggressive they will become.
- Aggressive children are slow to respond to warmth and praise but they need a great deal! Try to show them they give you pleasure simply by being themselves. By commenting *"I am enjoying playing this game with you,"* you make it explicit that you like them.
- They respond to being given responsibility.

- Help them to understand the impact of their behaviour. *"When you are angry, you make sure people remember you, but you maybe feel they don't like you very much."*
- Children in the group copy the playworkers' attitudes and behaviour. If you model an inclusive and understanding approach, the children will also slowly adapt a more tolerant approach to aggressive children at club.

The overwhelming child

Eleven year old David had moved to England with his parents during the summer holidays. He was a rather gangling child, slightly uncoordinated, occasionally peering over his rather thick spectacles in a comical way. He had had difficulty making friends in his native Canada, attributed to his general clumsiness and that he was not good at games. His parents were anxious for him to attend the after school club so *"He could practice his social skills."*

His playworker described how David first arrived at club. He had chatted with her awkwardly in a rather loud voice until another child entered the hall, then had bounded over to him with great enthusiasm, holding out his hand, bellowing, *"Hi, I'm David, you can be my friend."* Pushing his face far too close, he grabbed the astonished child's hand and shook it vigorously. David looked devastated when the other child pulled away and shrugged him off.

It was easy to understand why David had difficulty in getting on with other children: he was making grand, over-the-top overtures that overwhelmed the other children, who experienced him as aggressive, although it was not his intention to be aggressive. Bossy girls, typical of this age, often suffer the same problem—they don't understand they are being aggressive. As one girl said: *"I was just trying to make the game better."*

Excessive friendliness can be a solution to being very angry or frightened. David was feeling under pressure to socialise, fearing something was wrong with him because he didn't have any friends. His poor self-esteem was now making him go over the top in order to be friendly.

Managing overwhelming children

- Such children need help in imaging the effects of their behaviour on other children. Drama and role play can be as helpful as talking individually.
- Reassure such children that they are likeable. You could ask, *"What is there about you not to like?"*
- Explain that everyone has to learn to make friends. There is nothing wrong with them, it is just taking them a little longer than most people. Give them permission to learn social skills slowly, reassure them that it is alright to make mistakes.
- Help them to think of ways of putting things right when they do upset other children.

Grown-ups worry about children who can't get on with others. Of course, no one likes to see a child alone and ignored, casting as they do a bleak shadow of a future neglected adult. We are reminded of our deepest fear—of being disliked and rejected.

Socialising is a struggle, and perhaps the best we can do for children is help them to deal with the parts of themselves that are making the struggle harder.

HIDDEN MESSAGES—
BEHIND THE FAÇADE:
UNDERSTANDING
DISRUPTIVE CHILDREN

Children have limited ways of to
express themselves and also often don't
understand why they feel the way they
do—so playworkers need to try
discover what a child's behaviour
is really telling them

*"He's rude, a nuisance and he just spoils things for the others
. . ."*

Ten year old Ross was fast becoming the bane of his
play leader's life. *"He's our only problem,"* continued another
staff member, *"they'll all be getting on fine and then Ross
comes in and disrupts it all. The club is so different when he's
not aroun*d."

"Yes," added another, *"but he's fine one on one. It's when
he gets into a group he messes up."*

Feelings were running high in this staff support group;
it was obvious some of the staff wanted to exclude Ross,
not so much to punish him but because they simply didn't
know how to cope with him. They all shared the feeling
that they had used the gamut of their skills with him. Ross's
key worker tried to defend him: *"He's not a bad kid,"* she
said rather lamely, *"he's just disruptive."* Anyone working
with children would sympathise with these practitioners,
but are disruptive children *just* disruptive?

Disruptive children make adults feel helpless

Disruptive children are difficult to manage—by very virtue of their problem. They set out to disrupt—and that includes disrupting your management skills! So in a way the most difficult aspect of managing disruptive children is how they can make adults feel:

1. Powerless—"*I can't control him*".
2. Anxious—"*I'm supposed to be able to control him*".
3. Angry—firstly with the child for behaving so disruptively. Secondly, with ourselves for feeling powerless and anxious.

A disruptive child is an anxious child

Throughout this book we are thinking about how children use behaviour to communicate with grown-ups and how they often choose behaviour that makes the adult feel how they feel. Ross had a lot to be anxious about: he had little relationship with his father, who worked abroad for long periods at a time; his mother found it hard to cope alone with Ross, his two younger brothers, and a full-time job. Ross was always last to leave club, often saying his mother wouldn't be home "*till later*".

We could think of Ross as a "uncontained" child, a child full of overflowing worry. Structure is very important in helping children to feel contained: a regular routine with clear boundaries helps a child to be able to predict their day; they know roughly what is going to happen next. This mental and physical structure helps them to feel contained emotionally. Even if they are unhappy, the world may feel relatively safe because in a sense they know what is going to happen next. Ross never quite knew when his parents would be around, and his stressed mother ran a fairly *laissez-faire* home with irregular discipline and routine. One way of understanding Ross' disruptive behaviour was to think of him as looking for boundaries and containment. Being disruptive is a form of curiosity—it can be a way of finding out about authority. Here Ross was asking "*Where are the authority figures here, what will they allow and not allow?*" This is a very necessary developmental stage and, indeed, we can argue a little rebellion is no bad thing; maybe sometimes we should be more worried about children who don't test rules. However, disruptive children often don't understand a rule is a rule until they have broken it. They may not previously have had the experience of being told, in a firm but kind way: "this far and no further". And so in a sense, one of the things a disruptive child wants is to be prevented from being disruptive.

Disruptive children have often been disrupted

Ross's early life had been punctuated by frequent house moves and changes of school on account of his father's job. Additionally, his father's work was erratic, meaning he could be called abroad suddenly at short notice. Ross never really knew when he would and wouldn't see his father. As far as he was concerned, life could change dramatically at a moment's notice, and we can wonder what this means to a child.

Children often try to understand puzzling or worrying experiences by re-enacting them. For example, many of us have witnessed the scene where a toddler spills a drink on the carpet or the furniture. Initially shocked, the toddler then becomes fascinated by the adults' consternation, often watching intensely as the adults rush around trying to repair the damage. Then, seated again securely and encouraged not to spill another drink, the toddler may deliberately pour the second drink onto the carpet, usually causing outrage at their "naughtiness". Such a child isn't being naughty—they are more likely to be acting out the scene to try and understand it. What happened? Why were the adults so excited? Let's do it again and see if I can find out. So it is with the disruptive child—Ross was trying to make sense of disruptions in his life by reliving disruption over and over again.

Disruptive children are rarely "the *only* problem"

Disruptive children often work very hard on behalf of other children in the group. Their hard work often goes unrewarded! Earlier we were thinking about how in families one child can carry the feelings for everyone else, and the same process can happen in any group of children anywhere. (As indeed it does in staff groups!) Most of us have had the experience of being in a group where one person may be very negative about a child, and another person may be very positive about that child, feeling that however difficult the child is they have their good points. What happens dynamically is that because one person is holding the positive aspects of the child, other people in the group may feel free to be more negative about the child. Equally, sometimes when everybody is feeling very optimistic, one staff member may be left expressing all the negative points. In such a case, that staff member is carrying the negative aspects for the group, i.e., thinking about the aspects of the child the other members of the group find difficult to think about and experience.

Disruptive children sometimes are carrying disruption for the group. Ross was so disruptive the other children didn't need to be disruptive. If they felt discontent, angry, bored they didn't need to act on it because, unconsciously, they knew that Ross could be relied upon to express those feelings for them. It is often true that when a disruptive child is absent from a group for more than a very short period, a keenly observant play leader will notice that another child in the group becomes more "difficult".

When to worry

Disruptive and disturbing behaviour helps us to understand which children we should be worried about. The disruptive child is hoping that there is an adult around him who will eventually hear and take note of his anxieties. Much more worrying is the quiet and withdrawn child who may have given up on such a hope—these children can be overlooked because they are not disrupting the group or demanding the adults' attention.

Helping the disruptive child

Above all, a disruptive child needs to feel close to an adult, to feel attached to someone. In Ross' case, one play leader was assigned to take a special interest in him. She made sure that she always greeted him on arrival and that she checked on him at frequent intervals during club. His play leader was absolutely right when she said, "*He's alright one-on-one*". That may be exactly what Ross thought—in the early years he may have missed out on enough one-on-one attention from an adult and , so tended to feel a bit lost in a group.

Disruptive children need to feel secure. As soon as Ross arrived at after school club, his play leader made sure she explained to him very clearly exactly what was going to happen at club that evening. She made sure he knew exactly what the rules of any activity were, and exactly what would be expected of him if he joined in any activity. She also explained to him what he should do when he had finished an activity and tried to "pick him up" at the end of each activity so that his anxiety levels didn't get an opportunity to rise too high. The staff group as a whole tried to make an effort to keep checking on Ross every ten or fifteen minutes in a positive manner, by asking, *"Everything okay, Ross?"* or *"Having a good time, Ross?"*

Disruptive children need to feel contained by adults; they need to be able to rely on the routine of club as being relatively predictable and consistent. Play leaders are subject, of course, to the moods and stresses of everyday life, but children need them to be as consistent as they can be. However irritated they felt, Ross' play leaders tried to deal with his disruption in a calm, firm but kind manner. By doing so, they were giving Ross the message that however chaotic and disruptive he felt, he could not overwhelm the adults and deskill them; they could look after him and help him to manage his anxiety and chaos.

When we show children that we understand how they feel, and that we can help them to find a better way of communicating how they feel, then they learn not only how to get their needs met, but also how to respect other people. If you ask yourself *"How does this child make me feel?"* it will give you some understanding of how the child might be feeling, regardless of how he is behaving. Once you recognise how he feels, it will help you to respond to his behaviour. However, the question remains, who is going to contain adults looking after disruptive children?

SECRETS AND LIES:
WHY CHILDREN LIE

Should we take the same
approach to every child who tells
a lie, or should we first try to
understand why they
are lying?

Stephen, aged nine, was a worry to his club leaders. He regularly attended holiday club, and spent alternate weekends with his father, who was divorced from his mother. He boasted constantly to the other children about the exciting trips his father had taken him on and the grandness of his father's home. His club leaders knew the weekends with his father were much more ordinary than Stephen described. Some were irritated by his boasting and felt he needed to be confronted about it. Others did not want to risk humiliating him either in private or in public.

Another child in the same club, eleven year old Bea, had a different communication with her boasting. She was always telling her playworkers of her excellent ballet and music exam results. On one occasion she even boasted that she had come top of the section for her age group in ballet. This was a rather unfortunate claim as one of the playworkers' daughters held that position and her playworkers knew from her general lack of coordination that it was unlikely she was a star at ballet.

"That kid drives me mad . . . does he think I'm stupid the way he lies so blatantly?" Seven year old Wayne didn't make up stories, he just lied about trivial matters, usually around

whether or not he had completed tasks in club which could easily be checked up on.

When children lie, adults get angry. This is probably because, as Wayne's playworker highlights, we can feel outraged that a child thinks they can get away with it. However, there are also deeper issues for us; in many ways lying is an ordinary aspect of growing up for a child.

We can think of trivial lies like Wayne's as being a developmental stage. Such lies can be a child's way of checking up on how much the adults know about what they are doing when they are not around. When a young child gets away with a lie, they will be satisfied that they have a private life. Secrets and lies are an important way of a child establishing their independence and experimenting with separateness from their parents.

So why do adults get so angry about lying? Children are often punished not for the offence they have committed but for lying about it. We can attach huge importance to children not getting away with lying. Many playworkers will say that they feel that if they let a child get away with a small lie, then they run the risk of encouraging them implicitly into serious lying. This may reflect our fear that once a child begins to lie they are on a slippery slope.

Yet lying is also an ordinary aspect of adulthood. We make up excuses not to do things we don't want to do; we may try to convince other people we are wealthier than we are (or indeed happier than we are) in all sorts of ways such as buying clothes, cars and homes that we cannot really afford.

There are times in all our lives when we feel we need to both explain ourselves to other people and also to hide some aspects of ourselves. D.H. Lawrence suggested that we need to lie like we need to wear trousers.

Most people would label this kind of lie a "white lie" and see no harm in it; it is not serious lying, and white lies may often be told to protect someone else's feelings. However, maybe adults partly react so strongly to children lying because when a child lies to us it reminds us of a deep rooted human fear: the fear of being found out. But what is it that we fear will be found out? Just as adults deceive in different ways so do children and different lies at different ages can be communicating very different messages.

Lying over trivial matters

Wayne is typical of a seven year old using lying as a stage of development. However, if a child continues to tell trivial lies excessively after the age of seven, it is likely that the lying is less a stage of development and more a communication. Such a child may feel that they do not have enough age-appropriate freedom and that the adults are intruding too much into their growing private world. This is especially true of older children in club who are trying to develop a sense of privacy which excludes their parents.

Lying to exaggerate

Boasting lies may be a child's way of communicating their fear of rejection and also their way of experimenting with being a bigger and grander personality.

In thinking about Stephen we came to understand him as a child who felt he would only be popular if the other children envied him. He did not have a sense of being loved and admired simply for being himself; he felt he had to exaggerate his personality and life experience in order to be liked.

Bea had been trying to impress her playworkers with outstanding results in an attempt to gain their love, praise and recognition, which she felt were conditional on being competent. She was afraid that there was something wrong with "not knowing" or being incompetent. Such children live in a precarious world, putting themselves under extreme pressure to succeed for fear of losing love and approval.

The club workers began to think about the culture around incompetence both in these children's homes and in club. They reflected about how they reacted to their own mistakes. We often say "*I was so stupid . . . I was really dumb . . . I felt such a fool.*" Such responses may give children the impression that there is something wrong with making a mistake, rather than the idea that whilst one endeavours to do one's best in life, incompetence is part of being human.

Lying to describe how I feel

Eight year old Tamsin arrived one day at after school club very distressed. She explained that she had spilt orange juice on the carpet over the weekend and her mother had thrown away her favourite cuddly toy as punishment. She sobbed bitterly as she described that she had always slept with this cuddly toy since she was a baby.

Tamsin's playworker took her distress seriously and suggested that she could borrow another cuddly toy from club for a few nights. Privately she felt it was highly likely that Tamsin's mother would return the toy to her. However, when Tamsin continued to be upset for several days she raised the matter with her mother. It emerged that the story was complete fantasy on Tamsin's part.

In this book we are thinking about how children find it difficult to put their worries and unhappiness into words. Tamsin knew she felt sad but she didn't know how to explain her feelings to the adults.

Children like Tamsin may resort to a story which makes sense of their experience to them. An extreme situation is when a child may feel so unloved or abused by their parents that they say they are adopted because they feel their real parents would not treat them in such a way.

These fantasy lies are children's equivalent of adults using metaphors or similes to explain their feelings. For example, "*I felt like I'd been hit by a thunderbolt.*"

Tamsin's club leader realised it was important not to punish her for lying. She explained to Tamsin that she understood Tamsin was telling her that she felt as unhappy *as if* her mother had taken away her favourite toy as a punishment and no one cared or understood.

Dissociated lies—"It wasn't me"

Twelve year old Martin made his playworkers suspicious of him. He was an irregular member of after school club, but whenever he attended money, sweets, snacks and sometimes other children's possessions would disappear.

When these thefts were raised with the children Martin would look his playworker in the eye and steadfastly deny any involvement. He would also be extremely helpful in trying to give information which might trap the culprit. All the staff were convinced that Martin was the thief but they couldn't prove it. They also felt that Martin would be much more anxious when the thefts were discussed if he were guilty.

Eventually, Martin was caught red handed. He was immediately contrite and apologetic.

Sometimes children will mentally divorce themselves from the distressing or unhappy aspects of their life. In this way they will be able to hide their unhappiness and worry and appear to cope very well with life.

As a child you may well have had an imaginary friend whom you used as a scapegoat for your own misdemeanours. In a similar way, an older child may split off part of themselves, almost as though it is another person. What is split off is the aspects of themselves the child feels to be bad or unlovable.

Martin was trying to hide the worried and unhappy part of himself—the "bad Martin"—so that the adults would only be aware of the "good Martin". When such children are asked if they are lying, they will reply quite honestly "*No*," because they believe they are telling the truth. They have separated themselves from the person who *did* commit the offence.

Sometimes children like Martin can be persuaded to admit what they have done, but they are unlikely to understand adequately or accept the consequences of their behaviour. It is highly likely they will do the same thing again.

Children who tell dissociated lies are likely to need professional help. Once his stealing was discovered, Martin had to face the fact that there were not two Martins—a good one and a bad one—but only one Martin, who is a mixture of both the good and bad, the loveable and the unlovable. Once such children face this realisation they are likely to become depressed and more overtly unhappy.

131

STICKY FINGERS:
WHY CHILDREN STEAL

A child may steal not because
they want the object they have lifted,
but because they lack some basic
emotional fulfilment, which adults
can supply by helping them
to feel valued

Dylan, aged nine, struggled to explain his persistent stealing to his playworker. *"No, I know . . . it's not like I needed the stuff . . . it's like it fills up a hole."* As confused as Dylan, the playworker recounted the paltry objects he was stealing; the latest haul was typical: a felt tip pen, half a packet of sweets and the remnants of a ball of string.

At another club Martha, aged eleven, was stealing more valuable objects. She stole money from other children, from the staff, and also from her mother's purse. She would spend the money on quantities of sweets and chocolate bars which she then tried to share with other children. It was a puzzle to her playworkers how she could be so blatant, for within hours of a theft being discovered, Martha would turn up with a generous supply of goodies!

Playworkers are right to worry about petty stealing even though it is very common in childhood. A child who steals persistently is a worried child; they are worried because stealing is a desperate way of communicating with adults and because stealing makes a child feel powerless and out of control.

Stealing as a communication

Children like Dylan steal relatively worthless objects not because they need them, but to tell you that they fear they themselves are relatively worthless. in Dylan's words: *"Like there's a hole inside."* He was trying to explain that stealing is not about what he needed materially or what he wanted materially, it was about how he felt inside.

Dylan's mother had died when he was four years old and he was being brought up by his grandmother and his father. Dylan could not understand why his mother had died. Like many children suffering a loss, he blamed himself, worrying *"Did I do something to make her go away? Did she go away because she didn't love me any more?"*

By stealing worthless objects, Dylan was trying to tell the adults that he himself felt abandoned, like an unwanted thing. He had begun stealing about two years after his mother had died, when his father was given a promotion which involved his working away from home during the week. To Dylan it felt bewildering why his father would not want to be with him all the time.

Martha's stealing was a different kind of communication. She came from a difficult home where stress levels were high and time and affection at something of a premium. Her mother had always worked outside the home and Martha had had a series of childcare placements since she was six weeks old. We can think of her as feeling unloved, but deep down inside believing she *was* lovable.

She had worked out that other children liked her when she was giving out her sweets and chocolate—she was stealing to try to buy affection and popularity. As John Bowlby says, a lot of delinquent behaviour comes down to people trying to get close to each other. Martha did not need the sweets and chocolate she was stealing, what she did need was something emotionally that she felt she had never had.

Managing stealing

Dylan's key worker had been diffident about raising the matter with Dylan's grandmother; on one hand the items seemed too trivial to worry about, but on the other, their very lack of value, and the fact that Dylan seemed impelled to keep taking and hoarding them as treasure, was a cause for concern.

As it turned out, Dylan's grandmother was grateful that the staff spoke to her, as she was equally worried about Dylan at home. She said she would discuss the matter with his father. Imagine the playworker's horror when she told them on Monday morning that Dylan's father had grounded him for a week and threatened to "thrash him" if he didn't stop stealing at once. She approved of the father's approach, saying *"Where is this going to end? What's he going to take next? He's going to be delinquent!"*

It is unconstructive simply to punish a child for stealing. You need to make it clear to them that they cannot go on stealing mainly because stealing simply isn't working for them. Stealing is not getting them what they want or need and, indeed, is only making them feel worse about themselves. Children like Martha and Dylan feel even more worthless and unlovable once their stealing is discovered and they are punished.

Playworkers in both clubs found it difficult to accept that what these children needed was to be showered with spontaneous affection, kindness and treats. *"Surely this is just rewarding Martha for stealing?"* commented her key worker. Dylan's playworker pointed out that if Dylan was seen to go unpunished for stealing, it could only encourage other children in the group to steal.

There is a difference between managing a child kindly but firmly and colluding with unacceptable behaviour.

Children may find it difficult to distinguish between themselves and their behaviour, and so rather than saying *"I like you but not your behaviour,"* it may be more helpful to say, *"When you are stealing, we worry about you but we like you even when you are being this version of yourself."* This indicates to a child that their behaviour is part of them and that they are still loveable. That said, we need to set firm boundaries on a child's stealing, to explain to them that they steal because they feel bad inside, and to help them to think of other ways than stealing to feel better.

Martha's playworker encouraged her mother to try to give Martha some special one-on-one time on a regular basis. She had tried to do this the following weekend by taking Martha to the supermarket and buying her a drink and a chocolate biscuit afterwards. Martha seemed reluctant to eat the chocolate biscuit and asked if she could take it home; she seemed generally uneasy. She couldn't enjoy her special time because it seemed as if she felt like a criminal who had stolen something from her siblings.

We began to think of Martha as a child in a double bind. She felt that she and her siblings could only have quality time, affection, understanding and conversation with their mother at the expense of each other. It was as though she experienced these things as a cake, where if she had a slice, there was less left for everybody else.

We would hope that children grow up feeling that adults will want to give them to spontaneously. Children like

Martha may be afraid that anything good they receive is stolen. The risk for such children is that they may grow up finding it hard to enjoy successful relationships as adults; as soon as they become close to someone, they will feel overwhelmed with guilt that they are stealing the relationship from someone else.

Winnicott says that stealing can be understood as "a sign of hope". It can be argued that the greater the value of the things a child steals, the more hope there is for the child in the future! The child who steals is likely to be in a better state of mind, in that they believe they have a right to good things like time, admiration, and love and affection. Such a child is fighting for their place in the world. A similar child in the same position who doesn't steal could be understood as feeling too worthless to have any rights on other people.

Both Martha and Dylan responded well to their playworkers and family help. Had they not done so and their stealing had become compulsive, then they would have needed professional help. The child who steals compulsively is locked into a way of behaving which illustrates that they feel they can only get their needs met by stealing.

ROUGH AND TOUGH: BULLYING AND HOW TO PREVENT IT

Children who bully feel that
no one likes them. They try to
bully others into being their friends
but only succeed in making
matters worse. They need to be
shown kinder ways of
getting close

In May 2007 Suffolk became the latest county council in the UK to provide leaflets for children and parents on coping with bullying. We know that bullying is a growing problem for both children and adults in the UK today.

Bullying is not a new phenomenon. On the contrary, it seems to be an integral part of human relationships. In the past, adults and children alike had little recourse for help and indeed, a degree of bullying at school was considered not only normal, but even to some extent character building for children.

We are now much more sensitive to and informed about bullying and the impact it has on a person. Bullying goes against our basic human instinct to protect the weak and vulnerable, but we still have an ambivalent attitude towards it. An adult who slaps someone down may be applauded at work, for example. Accountability can easily turn into bullying for adults in the same way as the boundary between discipline and bullying is very often crossed by parents in the home.

All schools now have an anti-bullying policy and these have been so successful that there are reports now of bullies targeting their victims in more informal and less rigidly supervised settings: texting, for example, means a child can be bullied 24 hours a day. These new developments mean club workers are increasingly having to manage incidents of bullying in and around club. So how can we understand bullying?

Bullying as a way of trying to make friends

Nora's playworkers had noticed she was always on the fringe of friendship groups seemingly never fully accepted into any particular one. Now ten years old, she had attended after school club from Year 1. In the last year she had changed from being somewhat quiet and tearful to being more disruptive and bullying.

A parent had complained that Nora, who had been warned about bullying her daughter in club, was now sending the girl threatening text messages—up to about twenty in a day. *"It's 'cos she doesn't like me,"* sobbed Nora when asked to explain this most recent bullying. *"Do you think she likes you more now?"* replied her puzzled play-worker. *"No, nobody likes me, so I don't like anybody. But I'm the boss now."*

We need to hold in mind that bullies and their victims are in a passionate relationship. By this I mean there is no such thing as a random victim. Unconsciously, bullies and their victims are connected to each other; they both want something from the other.

I have described elsewhere (Clifford-Poston, 2007) how we can think of bullying as a friendship that can't find a way to work. In this sense, we can think of Nora wanting to be the friend of her victim, but not knowing how to be close to the other child. When she felt no one wanted to be her friend, she tried to bully children into friendships. She later admitted that she thought if she couldn't make people like her, then she would make them dislike her. Bullies want victims to be friends.

Bullying to get your point across

Nora's play leader observed how she coped quite well in twosomes. It was when she was in a larger group that the bullying arose. One scene was typical: Nora was in a group making a collage picture. She kept suggesting where pieces could go, but the other children never took up her suggestions. Eventually, she began to bully the younger child next to her into putting things where she said.

Nora felt ignored by the other children. She thought she could persuade the other children to her point of view by bullying them into taking notice of her. Adults do it all the time, raising their voice or thumping a desk. Children who bully may need help in finding more appropriate ways to persuade other people to their point of view.

Bullying to make me feel better

Nora was asked to explain how she thought her victim felt. Nora looked ashamed but said she didn't know. Her play leader spelt out that the other girl was feeling *"bad and unhappy."* Nora burst out *"I'm glad 'cos I feel bad and unhappy."*

Bullying is about one person feeling powerful and the other feeling dominated. Most of the time Nora felt lonely and unhappy. Like many bullies she had previously been a victim. Her play leader remembered how viciously Nora's elder sister had treated her. This is how whole families can get a reputation as bullies and can be written off as such by the community.

Nora wanted to stop feeling bad and unhappy. At a very deep level, she thought if she could push her painful feelings into another child by bullying them, she would feel less dominated by those feelings.

Of course, there is a sense in which Nora did feel better temporarily: as a bully she felt strong and powerful, but her feelings of being disliked and isolated only increased, causing her to seek more victims.

Helping the bully

Children who bully are trying to draw an adult's attention to their unhappiness. Paradoxically they are telling the adults this is how they feel: dominated and powerless. No child should ever be allowed to bully another—this is not only in the victim's interest but also in that of the bully. Bullies are always relieved when they are prevented from bullying. Remember: Nora wanted friends, not victims.

The most difficult part of managing a bully is the impact they have on the adult. Bullying children make us want to come down hard on them, to isolate them often; indeed, to bully them into stopping bullying! It is a fine line for a play leader, in the hurly-burly of a busy day, to distinguish between being firm but kind with a child, and to bully them into behaving in a different way. Of course, such treatment can only make a bully feel even more power-less and, therefore, more likely to bully again.

- Give a clear, firm but kind message that the adults will not allow them to bully.
- Help them to think about their victim—what do they like about their victim? What do they think the victim likes about them? This is different to making the bully feel guilty and bad with angry exhortations such as *"How would you like it?"*
- Help them to think of more appropriate ways of getting what they want from other children. For example, how else could Nora have persuaded the group to agree with her point of view?

Understanding victims

Why are some children more bullied than others? Some children try to be an irritant to others—*"Mind you, she asked for it,"* is often the irritated last phrase in any adult's description of the frequently bullied child. As one twelve year old tried to explain, *"When they* [other children] *bully me I'm not a Nicky no-mates."* He preferred to be bullied by other children to feeling unnoticed on the fringe of the group. But, of course, both feelings left him unhappy and anxious.

Children who invite bullying are making themselves a nuisance to somebody else and that may be a very important communication for them.

Helping the victim

When Nora bullied, she was trying to force other children to comply with her demands. A forceful child cannot become a bully if the other children know how to stand firm against them.

- Encourage a victim to talk about being bullied and not to feel ashamed of it.
- Reinforce to the child that it is not their fault they are being bullied.
- Show gentle and mild curiosity in their predicament. Ask them, *"I wonder what it is about you that makes so and so want to bully you?"* Without blaming, a child can be helped to think about their part in the bully/victim relationship.
- Ask yourself, *"How does this child know when he has made an impact on other people?"*
- Help the child to think about more effective ways to make an impact on other people.

Preventing bullying

Can we prevent bullying? Maybe not entirely, but we can create an environment in which bullying is not encouraged and not tolerated.

- Staff need to work out a clear definition of bullying. There can be a fine line between teasing and bullying. Teasing can be fun, teasing can also be very cruel. Staff need to be able to spot the most subtle signs of bullying as early as possible.
- Be as worried about the victim as the bully. Assume both the bully and the victim are really quite unhappy. Bullying is always a sign that someone is feeling power-less, confused, or bullied themselves.

- Play leaders and parents may need to team up to help both a bully and a victim. Talking to parents about their child's bullying is a delicate task. The risk of complaining to parents that their child is bullying is that the parents may respond defensively, or they may become angry and try to discipline the child into not bullying. A gentle approach, such as: *"He seems a bit unsettled in after school club—have you noticed any changes in his behaviour at home?"* may invite parents to think about their child's predicament. Avoid conversations of "persuasion". Trying to persuade a parent that their child's behaviour is worrying may make them only more defensive. If you feel you are reaching a stalemate, try saying something like *"Well, we don't have to agree about this, but we are very concerned about him at after school club."*

Think about staff relationships

Children learn how to treat other people from the adults around them. Siblings who fight and argue excessively may be replicating their parents' arguing relationship. And so it is in after school clubs: children will be acutely aware of, and sensitive to, how you as a staff relate to each other. If you treat each other (and the children!) with respect, tolerance and understanding, you will create an environment where children have a strong chance of feeling heard, understood and cared for, and when any one of us feels that, we have no need to bully.

HIT AND RUN:
HAPPY SLAPPING

Happy slapping is not just
notoriety-seeking, copy-cat behaviour,
but a re-enactment of the humiliation
of others youngsters see around them
everyday, and is a form of bullying

Two eleven year old girls left their after school club around 5pm to walk ten minutes round the corner to meet the older brother of one who was going to escort them home. It was dark but the streets were well lit and it was a relatively quiet residential area.

As they waited at the meeting point they noticed a small group of slightly older youngsters who attended their school walking towards them. As the group passed the girls, one boy turned and hit them, one after the other, hard on the head. As they reeled in shock, they became aware of the rest of the group laughing and jeering further up the road as one filmed the attack on his mobile phone. Both girls were hit several times before their attacker cried to his friends, *"Did you get it?"* and ran off.

The distressed girls decided to run back to the club where their leaders were horrified when they recognised this latest incident of "happy slapping".

What is happy slapping?

If ever there was a misnomer it is the phrase "happy slapping". It conjures up a picture of innocent fun, perhaps even of a congratulatory and friendly nature. Nothing could be further from the truth.

Happy slapping is a craze gathering pace in this country; a group of youngsters gang up on a victim, who may be an innocent bystander or passer-by, and assault them with sudden slaps around the head while other members of the group use their mobile phones to video the attack. Videos of the slaps are then exchanged around mobile phones and, in some cases, even posted on the internet.

Police and anti-bullying organisations have reported that this teenage fad, which began in south London in late 2004, has now become a nationwide phenomena. Although club aged children are more likely to be the victims than the perpetrators of happy slapping, club workers are right to be concerned that the craze could quickly move from the playground to club. They are all too aware how ordinary bullying by a group can escalate into something more sinister.

It is important that we try to understand what it is a youngster feels they are gaining by taking part in happy slapping, as well as thinking about how to help the victim.

The desire for celebrity status

In May 2005 Dr Graham Barnfield, Head of Media at the University of East London, said in a television interview with Trevor McDonald that he felt the craze was rooted in TV shows such as *Jackass* and *Dirty Sanchez*, which show youngsters "attacking" passers-by while recording the incident on their mobile phones. The "victims" have volunteered to be "surprised" on television.

145

He explained, "*I think 'happy slapping' has become a short cut, in the eyes of the slappers, to fame and notoriety among the people who see the images circulated on the web or sent to them via their mobile phones.*"

In the same programme, a sixteen year old slapper described how "*You see someone just sitting there, they look like they're dumb, you just run up to them and slap them, and run off. It's funny.*"

But it is not only on television that children observe sado-masochistic behaviour. Many children will have seen their parents goading or tormenting each other. They are likely to have been teased or bullied by their siblings. Children try to make sense of puzzling behaviour by re-enacting or playing it out. Perhaps at a very deep level, happy slappers are trying to show us something about family life. We could argue they are trying to tell adults that there is something wrong in our society and no one seems able, or willing, to do anything to remedy it. And they are right.

We see people shaming and humiliating others as part of our everyday life: be it Allied troops humiliating Iraqi prisoners, or journalists searching for murky details on the private lives of almost anyone in the public eye. Children themselves are taking up the fashion. " *'Fess up and take the shame,*" they say to each other. "Take the shame" has a very different ring to an encouragement to own up and take responsibility for one's actions.

We seem to almost have a sense of glee in seeing someone shamed; how else can we explain the extraordinary viewing figures for *Big Brother*, a programme which sets out to humiliate and shame its participants. So we can wonder what is the purpose of shame in our society today.

The power of the group

Sometimes happy slapping attacks will be planned events in schools or the playground and on such occasions a huge crowd of children are likely to emerge from nowhere to watch the incident. The majority of observers will be, on the whole, responsible youngsters, so what happens to them in these group events that they begin to behave in a totally uncharacteristic way? The two girls at the beginning of this chapter knew their assailants. Indeed, the boy videoing the happy slapping was a friend of the brother and had always been warm and friendly when visiting the family home.

We are all capable of being violent towards other people. Most of the time we control our aggression, consciously or unconsciously, because we have been taught not to harm other people and because we want to think of ourselves as "good people". However, it is relatively easy to feel anonymous in a group. It is easy to feel "innocent" in a group. We can claim either that we weren't actually "doing it", we were only observing other people doing it, or we were made to do it by the group!

In groups, people give themselves permission or provide themselves with an opportunity to abandon control and inhibitions and to behave in a way that is normally so repressed we may not even be aware we were capable of behaving in such a way. For children, entering a group can feel rather like entering a world without adults. Unconsciously, they feel they can experiment with behaving in a way that would normally be forbidden by the presence of adults. And sadly, what we know from world history (and William Golding's novel *Lord of the Flies*), is that when human beings feel free from constraints, they become sadistic to each other. Once cruelty begins in a group, it takes enormous courage and strength of character for any one person to protest against it.

Passing on the pain

Happy slapping is not funny: it is bullying. It is traumatic for its victims both physically and emotionally. As I said in the previous chapter, bullying has many faces but it always involves the strong picking on the weak. The heart of bullying lies in a power/domination relationship.

As I have said earlier, at the deepest level, a bully dreads feeling afraid, alone or isolated. Bullying can be a way of passing on our pain to someone else in an attempt to feel strong and powerful, rather than vulnerable. So we can think of the boy who happy slapped the two eleven year old girls as temporarily feeling strong and powerful, encouraged and admired by his mates. Perhaps he needed this experience as a solution to feeling isolated and afraid most of the time because of his own experiences with a violent father. Like all human beings, he had the capacity to be violent and when he suffered violence he needed to get rid of his feelings of pain and shame. The current social milieu of happy slapping provided him with the opportunity to act out his aggression.

Thumping and slapping each other is common behaviour amongst the 12+ age range. They use it as a way of expressing both affection for and anxieties about each other. It is especially common between boys and girls, almost a way of making contact without allowing closeness.

As professionals, we need to be able to see the signs when this normal behaviour has stepped over a boundary into bullying or "happy slapping" and to create an environment in which youngsters feel able to tell us what is happening.

PART FIVE:
SPECIAL NEEDS?

BEST MATES

Why is it so important to some children to have a best friend, and do all such friendships form for the same reason? Can they get in the way of the adults trying to run an out-of-school club? Let us consider some of the rules of attraction

In the first eight years or so of children's lives, their friendships tend to be orchestrated by their parents. Children's first friends are often the offspring of their parents' friends and even later on when friendships are formed at school, both sets of parents are likely to know each other. These early friendships are also likely to be lived out in the home in the sense that small children do not go out alone with their friends. Significant changes take place in friendships at the onset of the "betweenage" (pre-teenage) years. Many nine year olds are not only beginning to make friends independent of the family's circle of friends but are also becoming aware of shades and degrees of friendships. They will understand the difference between, as one nine year old described, *"There are friends like with everyone in the class and then there's special friends that you do things with."* This girl was longing to have "a best friend" and because she didn't have a best friend she considered herself "Nicky-no-mates."

We are right to be concerned about a nine year old who has difficulty in making friends, but should we worry about a child who does not have a best friend? And what does it mean to a club aged child to have "a best friend"?

151

Being popular versus having friends

Eleven year old Lauren's playworkers were concerned about her. She had been attending after school club for three years and initially she had seemed happy and settled, but over the past eighteen months she had become increasingly sad and irritable. "*She's a very popular girl*," said her key worker, "*there is no problem with friendships.*"

Popularity does not necessarily equate with friendships. Lauren was a popular girl because her wealthy parents could afford lavish treats—she always had the latest of everything and her parents were generous to other children in an attempt to support her friendships. So from an adult's point of view, Lauren was always surrounded by other children and did not seem isolated; but Lauren saw things differently. She felt she hadn't got a "real friend" or a best friend and tried to explain to her club worker that while she was constantly inviting other children out at weekends nobody ever invited her, unless it was a class or a large group event.

Children can be popular for all sorts of reasons and popularity is not necessarily an indication of the quality of their relationships.

What is a best friend?

Many adults seem to need not only a circle of friends but also a particular friend with whom they enjoy a special sense of empathy, affinity and trust. Some children may share this need—like the ten year old who, when asked to define the difference between a best friend and other friends, said "*A friend is someone who knows you and likes you and you like them. A best friend is someone who really knows you and really likes you.*"

Other children may have a much more nonchalant view, like the twelve year old who saw a best friend as "*Someone you see more often. It doesn't mean you like them better, you just see them more.*" Betweenagers need a group of friends to whom they feel they belong and with whom they can share interests and practice identities, but a "best friend" may not be crucial.

Attraction of opposites

Friends introduce children to change and diversity. They introduce each other to difference—be it interests, ways of doing things, cultures or food. One eight year old was astonished to find his friend was allowed to eat meals on his lap watching TV: "*He doesn't have to sit at the table with his mum and dad!*" More poignantly, another boy noted that his friend's father "*Never yells at him.*"

Sometimes a best friend can be an alter ego for a child: someone who lives their unlived life. Ben and James formed an intense friendship at holiday club much to the concern of Ben's parents. Ben was a quiet, well behaved and diligent nine year old. Eleven year old James could not have been more different—he was loud and brash, openly defiant and known to wander the streets after dark with a gang of older boys. Ben's parents felt he was a bad influence on their son and wanted club workers to keep the boys apart as much as possible.

The playworkers' initial reaction was to agree with Ben's parents but as they reflected on the friendship they were less sure that the boys needed to be kept apart. In the weeks they had been friends neither James's nor Ben's behaviour had changed. Ben was just as cooperative, James was just as belligerent. They were clearly happy and lively in each other's company but they did not seem to be influencing each other's behaviour. Ben said he liked James because he was *"Well wicked—he knows what to do."* James, on the other hand, thought Ben was *"Cool,"* because *"he does really interesting stuff."* Friendships are often based on curiosity at this stage. Ben secretly admired James because he was able to defy the adults, something Ben didn't dare to do. James on the other hand was curious about how Ben managed to have a good time and not annoy the adults. We can think of their friendship as being based on their being curious about how it would feel to be more like each other.

We need to remember also that friends are "chosen" siblings. Children will often choose a friend to help them work out a relationship with a sibling or to help them to understand what it would have been like to have a sibling, or to have a different kind of sibling.

Similar friends

Jack and Ben were a different kind of best friends. They had met at a Saturday morning club for gifted children in an inner city area. They quickly discovered that they shared a passionate interest in insect life and finding someone to share this interest made a dramatic difference to their self-esteem. Jack explained, *"At my school, I'm just a sad geek, but now I feel I'm the same as someone else."*

Club aged children are beginning to think about how to separate from their family. In order to do so, they have to establish their own identity as a distinct and unique person in their own right. This can be a terrifying process and having a best friend who is "all the same" can be a solution to the fear "I don't know who I am." As Ben said, *"I know I am me, i.e., identifiable as an eleven year old boy with an interest in insects because I have a friend who is also interested in insects. But when no one else was interested in insects then I used to wonder who I am."*

Wanting a best friend

"I can't do anything, can I? I mean I can't go out or anything because I haven't got a best friend to go with." Twelve year old Jason illustrates how friends can be so important to his age group that they may fear it is impossible to enjoy any activity alone. No one likes to see a child feeling friendless and lonely. But making friends is rather like falling in love, you can't be taught to do it, you just have to put yourself into circulation and let it happen. However, you can help such a child to reflect on their part in making friends by asking them what they think it is about them that stops someone being their best friend. Jason gave an interesting reply to this question: *"Well, I'm a bit bossy, I like to be in charge and the others don't like that."* When mixing with other children Jason had lots of good ideas about what they should do and how a game could develop. In talking things through, Jason and his playworker were able to think of ways Jason could put his good ideas across to other children without seeming to be bossy. This helped him to think about what there was about him other children may like, and that if they liked him, they may want him to be their best friend.

Falling out

Sally and Emma had fallen out again! "*I have to be the same as Sally or she hates me and gets mad and tells everyone else not to be my friend,*" explained Emma to her playworker. There seems to be a sex difference in the nature of friendships of children of this age. Boys tend to play together in groups centred around a common interest, often of sport. Girls' friendships tend to centre around sharing confidences—the more secrets shared, the closer the friendship. This may be why girls are more likely to form friendships in threesomes— a particular feature of girl friendships at this age.

Threesomes provide girls with an opportunity to explore issues of power and status. It is likely that one of the three is always going to be feeling left out or one is demanding that the other two can't be friends with each other and with her. Girls can become very possessive of each other, feeling intimacy and loyalty have to be exclusive. They can be very demanding of a best friend and can push the relationship to its limits by insisting "sameness" on every issue within the friendship.

Adults can be very frustrated by these relationships. We can be drawn into spending time and energy in trying to understand the nature of the quarrel only to find that two hours later the girls are the best of friends again! Remember:

- Learning to deal with being left out is part of growing up.
- Children's friendships are like adult relationships in that they are not necessarily permanent, they run their course.
- Resist the urge to orchestrate children's friendships. It may be more important to help them to think of ways of sorting things out with their friends.

YOU'VE GOT MALES:
UNDERSTANDING BOYS

But how can playworkers deal with play fighting that becomes aggressive? How can we understand what lies behind that male swagger?

Aged eleven, Sam had learnt to swagger. He had perfected swaggering: his head held high, chin jutting, his face gleaming with self-satisfaction. He swaggered into after school club, hands in pockets, arms akimbo, hips swinging as he approached a group of children already involved in activities. As he reached his best friend in the group, he thumped him hard on the back with his elbow (though without removing his hands from his pockets!) His friend responded with a sharp backward kick on the shin— almost at once two playworkers marched over and pounced on Sam, aggressively reprimanding *him* for being aggressive.

Why do we worry about boys' aggression, which, let's face it, can often be less hurtful than the vituperative tongues of some girls of this age? As an observer, it seemed clear to me that Sam and his friends were about to have a play fight. "Play fight" is exactly what it says, a time when boys experiment with aggression and practice their strength and power. They seem to do this instinctively, as soon as they reach school age, in rough and tumble play with each other and any other male who will take them on. They roar around kicking, hitting, swinging and climbing. So why do adults rush in to stop play fighting? "*Well*", said Sam's play leader, "*play fighting can lead to real fighting and then someone gets hurt.*"

Recent research by the London Metropolitan University has shown that boys in nurseries who are allowed to fight and play with toy guns, on the whole, do not hurt each other too much and also develop close friendships. But adults worry about boys fighting. Could this be because in play children reflect how men and women behave towards each other? Stopping boys' aggressive play may be our way of saying *"We don't want you to grow up to be like us—prone to violence and aggression."*

Demonstrating affection

During the 1960s and 70s there was a huge growth in the feminine and pacifist movements. At this time, qualities such as sensitivity and kindness were identified as female. Why? Can males not also be sensitive and kind? Boys have inherited a fundamental dilemma. Boys have a mother and a father; they want to be like both parents. It has become quite a task for them to find a way of being like their mothers, when feminine qualities can be experienced as compromising their masculinity. How, for example, can boys show each other affection?

Girls of this age are famous for their intense friendships, in which they share secrets and are physically very affectionate. Boys are just as fond of their friends but tend to be more awkward and embarrassed about expressing affection. Sam was typical: greeting his friend with a shove. Boys may show affection by pushing, shoving, thumping and rolling all over the floor like puppies. So often what looks like aggression is actually the boys' equivalent of girls' walking around with their arms round each other.

The fact that this affectionate "play fighting" may lead to real fighting and someone getting hurt is not necessarily "a bad thing", for in play fighting boys are also trying to find the limit and extent of their body power. They are acting out serious anxieties for them at this age—how strong am I? Who is stronger than me? How does it feel to hurt and to be hurt . . . to be the conqueror, to be the victim? To see this play only in terms of "male competitiveness" is mistaken. Boys learn to be boys by being allowed to practice being male.

That we do not consider play fighting to be as pretty or as endearing a sight as the affectionate whispering and cuddling of girls' friendships is our problem, not the boys'. Girls find their pecking order much more subtly, by choosing with whom they will and will not share secrets. The more secrets a girl carries, the higher she is up the pecking order. The risk of constantly asking boys to stop fighting or being rough is that they may begin to feel that there is something bad about being a boy. They are behaving as nature intended, but they may get a message that it is better to do things the girls' way. So boys may be left with a problem of how to be a good boy and be male.

What we call aggression we can also call vitality. Asking boys not to be so aggressive can feel like asking them not to be so alive. And it is interesting that girls' twittering in huddles can be just as irritating to adults as boys rolling all over the floor knocking over the furniture.

Sam's swaggering irritated his play leader. She saw it as aggressive, sullen, rude and even threatening. "*You have to come down hard on him,*" she said. "*You can tell by the way he swaggers in, he's out for trouble.*" Later in the year, a male student—Dave—was spending time in the club. At the end of his first week, Sam swaggered up behind him (almost into him!) and, raising his hand, he greeted the turning Dave with a meeting of palms in a high-five, shouting

"Yo! 'Sup, Dave?"

"Yo! Yo! Sam," replied Dave, "'sup Sam?"

In this book we are constantly thinking about how naughtiness is very much a matter of how behaviour is construed. Dave regarded Sam with a mixture of amusement and affection as he watched him trying to swagger into being a "cool" man. His play leader was astonished at both Dave's management and Sam's response. Boys will sometimes put on a tough, aggressive front as a way of trying to cover an anxiety and insecurity about being liked and likeable. At this age, boys want to be admired for being male.

Sam wasn't being rough or a bully, or even looking for trouble, he was practising being a man. And during this exuberant rehearsal he was bound to accidentally knock people over or even hurt them. He was also bound to knock things over and even break them. But demonising him as his play leader did, and meeting his aggression with aggression, simply reinforced for him the idea that there was something wrong with being a boy. When Sam's play leader was tough on him, he understood this as an invitation to take her on. He became more "male" in his behaviour in an unconscious attempt to show her what a man he was becoming. In the same way, an eleven year old girl told not to wear eye shadow in club may well appear the next day wearing lip gloss and nail polish to prove she is female.

Rare species

We can sympathise with Sam's play leader's behaviour. The lack of male play leaders in clubs means boys often only have women on whom to test out their masculinity. Boys of this age can feel very threatening to female workers. Consciously, or unconsciously, their behaviour can say, "I'm rejecting what you stand for" i.e., all things female. It is then all too easy for women play leaders to get caught up in the boys' struggle. Responding aggressively to aggressive boys can be a way of insisting, women are valuable, too!

Boys are naturally high-spirited and boisterous. They need to be provided with activities which allow them to let off steam. Years ago this used to happen naturally as children ran free and played outside. Another restriction is that sport has been downgraded in importance in schools. In some areas, club may be one of the few places where boys can find a safe environment to develop their male identities. We know that boys who are allowed to expend energy in some rough and tumble play concentrate better and are more well behaved in following later quieter activities.

Of course, in club, the adults are there to protect the children. Boys' rough and tumble play needs to be carefully monitored and there should be zero tolerance on bullying and viciousness.

Maybe our focus on boys' aggressive behaviour is missing the point. We seem to have developed the idea of segregating life into "boys do . . ." and "girls do . . ." We should argue that vitality and sensitivity are issues for both boys and girls. We can argue that if boys were freer to be gentle, sensitive and kind, then girls would feel freer to be more ruthlessly aggressive. Perhaps we should not be worrying so much about persuading boys to be less aggressive, and worrying more about encouraging girls to be more vital?

ALL INCLUSIVE: THE CHILD WITH SPECIAL NEEDS

Welcoming a child with special needs to a club may cause anxiety for the child and parents and lead staff to question their skills

Ten year old Sarah had long wanted to join after school club with her younger brother. Although her cerebral palsy meant she had indistinct speech and used a wheelchair she had always attended mainstream school with the support of a non-teaching assistant. Now she was becoming aware of her friends' steps to independence and was nagging her parents to let her attend club. As the staff made their plans to receive her a number of interesting points about inclusion came to the surface.

Understanding the parents

The staff liked Sarah's parents. They had known them both since her brother had joined club a year previously. But now they noticed a change in them as preparations were being made for Sarah to come along as well. They began to comment on incidents such as the time during a game of table tennis when a child hit the ball so hard he also let go of the bat, which flew across the room and hit another child. There were no serious injuries and no complaints at the time, and although Sarah's parents' tone was kindly enough, the staff felt mildly irritated that they were raising this now as a potentially dangerous situation for Sarah; it was, after all, a one-off accident.

Many parents feel concerned as their child takes their first steps into the outside world. It is natural enough that this sense of anxiety is highlighted for parents when a child has special needs. First and foremost, playworkers have to recognise and understand the anxiety of parents like Sarah's. Some parents in their position would be anxious about the child's safety and ability to cope. In Sarah's case this was less so because her carer would be going to club with her. But, of course, this new step for Sarah was highlighting her parents' anxiety about how she was going to cope with life as a teenager.

Parents show their anxiety in a myriad of ways, perhaps checking every detail is in place obsessively before the child starts club, or demanding very special arrangements which may be difficult for club to provide. It is easy for club workers to be left feeling criticised, incompetent or even uncaring in the face of a parent's anxiety. We need to bear in mind constantly what a stressful time joining club may be for the parents.

Impact on the staff

The phrase "special needs" is an ambiguous one; whilst it accurately describes Sarah's predicament, there is a risk that it sets her apart. Sarah's assigned key worker seemed particularly anxious and worried the day before Sarah arrived. "*What if I can't manage her? What if I don't understand her?*" She was a highly experienced playworker but here she was feeling deskilled by Sarah's "special needs."

While it was true that there were certain different physical needs (in terms of toileting, for example), Sarah's main needs in club were exactly the same as any other ten

163

year old's. In this sense, there was nothing about Sarah's needs her playworker did not know. But disability raises all sorts of anxieties about the unknown and the different. It is a human enough reaction to be anxious because we may not understand something or someone new and different.

Anxiety as a communication

Sarah's arrival in club went well—she settled quickly and seemed relaxed and happy during her first few days, so I was surprised to find not only Sarah's key worker, but also the other playworkers, feeling worried and anxious by the end of the second week.

They found it difficult to put their anxiety into words. "*Sarah seems almost too confident,*" said her playworker. We thought about what overconfidence might be a solution to and what might be being communicated. We remembered again that when children cannot put their feelings into words they may fall back on projection to let the adult know how they are feeling. Children's feelings are raw and primitive and it can be difficult not to be overwhelmed by them. Once the staff began to think of Sarah, and perhaps the other children, feeling anxious and worried, their own anxiety began to decrease and they were able to think creatively. It is difficult to admit to our anxieties or fears of not coping and particularly so for a child with a disability, who may feel they have to do twice as well as the others to get on in life. They may also have grown up feeling praised and admired for the way they cope. Asking yourself "*How does this child make* me *feel?*" may give you a real insight into how the child with special needs is feeling.

Disability gets into the system

Sarah attended a very well run club with a professional staff. Several weeks after she joined her playworker reported an interesting incident. The club was going to a local beauty spot for an afternoon picnic. The playworker had been shocked to discover on the arranged day that she had booked the coach for the following day. The trip was rearranged for the next week when, to her absolute horror, she realised she had booked the coach to arrive at the collection time! This was so unlike her everyone was bewildered.

In any group of people there is an unconscious dynamic which sometimes lodges in one or more member of the group. We thought earlier about how we have all had the experience of being in a jocular group which has grown flat and dissipated when a more depressed person has joined it. It is not uncommon for people working with someone with a disability to sometimes find themselves "disabled" in their skills and management. At an unconscious level, we sometimes have to carry the disability for the child so that they are free to succeed. The risk here is people will feel critical of themselves or others for being incompetent, rather than understanding that sometimes disability gets into the system.

Impact on the child

Before Sarah joined club her playworkers discussed at length with her parents the nature of her disability and also how much Sarah herself knew about her disability. Sometimes staff are reluctant to do this because they feel there is a risk of defining the child by their disability. Whilst this can happen, we can also argue that it is essential for staff to know what impact a child's disability is going to have on their club life.

What a child understands about their disability colours the way in which they see the world as much as their physical problems. If we ask a blind child and a deaf child to describe a thunder storm they experienced together, the blind child is likely to describe thunder and the deaf child is likely to describe lightning; they have a very different reality about the same experience.

Learning as much as possible about the child's disability is as much a way of getting to know the child as an individual as is seeing beyond the disability to the individual child.

Building confidence

The staff were understandably anxious to help build Sarah's confidence. The best way was to be as realistic as possible with her. There should be no mysteries about her or surrounding her. For this reason the staff felt it was important to try not to hide the fact that Sarah was different. For example, when she seemed sad or anxious about activities, such as disco dancing, which she could not join in in the same way as other children, the staff resisted the temptation to distract her with comments like, "*Oh, but you are so good at table tennis,*" but focussed on her feelings, by saying something like, "*It is disappointing that you have to be in a wheelchair . . .*" and then seeing where she took the conversation.

Later on, you can draw attention to other qualities and abilities if it feels appropriate as a way of highlighting for a child with a disability that they may have things that other children would like to have.

The risk of teasing

Teasing is part of everyday life and you may not be able to prevent it. However, children are most influenced in their attitude towards each other by the behaviour and attitudes of the adults around them. Staff can do much to foster a general attitude of respect and tolerance in club and, in particular, towards those who may seem a little different.

It is important to be aware of envy when a child with a disability is present. Some children will be envious of the special attention children like Sarah receive. Equally, Sarah was gradually able to voice her envy of the other children's relative freedom. Sometimes envy is expressed as teasing or bullying.

Acceptance as an equal

All children use their abilities and disabilities to their own advantage. Everyone wanted to help Sarah, sometimes doing things for her that she was clearly able to do herself. Overprotection stunts children's curiosity and independence. Staff needed to watch that Sarah did not become the "club pet." Other children were encouraged to accept her as an equal who may sometimes need a little extra help. Otherwise, Sarah could grow up feeling the only way to cope with life is to be helpless and helped. Her confidence grew as she realised there were many things she could achieve at the same level as other children.

We need to remember "special needs" are exactly what they say—unique and special to each child. In club, each child will experience another's disability individually. For

167

example, a child with a younger sibling may regard Sarah simply as someone needing a bit of extra help like a younger child. They may feel relaxed or irritated by this depending on their relationship with their sibling. No two children with younger siblings will necessarily experience a child with special needs in the same way. However, there will be an unconscious peer pressure to "agree" on disability just as there is an unconscious peer pressure to agree on any child in the group be it "the bright one" or "the pretty one" and so on. Workers need to be alert to each child's unique understanding of what it is like to have a disability.

BRAINPOWER: UNDERSTANDING GIFTED CHILDREN

Play leaders may feel anxious if a "gifted" child is to join their club, but there are positive ways to ensure the child is accepted

Club enhances children's lives in many ways, perhaps mostly by encouraging them to be themselves, to develop their own particular gifts and skills, and valuing them for both. So I was surprised at the anxiety level in a staff support group as ten year old Tara was being discussed.

Tara was joining club the next day. "*She's gifted—a bit of a brain box,*" said one worker with a nervous smile. Tara's teachers and parents were concerned that she was isolated from her peer group at school; she had no particular friend and the other children certainly regarded her as odd. The hope was that after school club would help her to socialise. Helping children to socialise is the essence of a playworker's work, so why were the staff anxious?

"*Well, can we meet her needs?*" commented one, provoking a torrent of worries to pour out. "*It's difficult to know how to plan for her,*" summed up another. When I asked what would be different if they had known only that Tara needed help to socialise and not that she was gifted, everyone immediately relaxed, feeling that in such a case there would be no problem.

What is a gifted child?

Adults tend to need to label children. It seems difficult for us to accept a child as the sum of their parts and to think of them holistically, especially when they are difficult for us to manage. Of course nowadays a child needs a label to qualify for any special need and in that sense a label works in the child's best interests. However, in Tara's case the label was in a sense alienating, in that the staff felt temporarily deskilled and unable to think beyond the label. Indeed, blinded by the word "gifted" they had lost track of their own giftedness in helping children to socialise.

A gifted child is an ordinary child with an extraordinary talent; they come in all sorts of shapes and sizes: they may have a superior intelligence or a particular outstanding talent. They may be socially gifted, which is generally seen as an asset rather than a problem. While being gifted doesn't automatically cause a problem for a child, it does raise the question how much does a child's gift link them to other people and how much does it separate them from other people?

Impact on the child

Tara could not remember when she didn't feel different to other children. As a small child she felt special, as her precociousness earned her a good deal of adult approval. At the end of her first term in school she was moved up a class, which met some of her academic needs but emotionally exaggerated her sense of being different. She knew she pleased her teachers, she was less confident about how to please her peers and how to make friends. The more she felt she didn't belong, the more she turned towards adults for "friendship" by becoming a rather loud "know all" in class. Challenging behaviour can sometimes be an indication of giftedness, as indeed can withdrawn behaviour. Both may indicate that a child's needs are not being met.

Tara experienced a common dilemma of gifted children. In a sense she was becoming bewitched by her giftedness, believing her "super brain power" was the primary and most important aspect of her. She seemed unaware of her other admirable qualities and believed people liked her *solely* because she was gifted intellectually. Her feelings of being special and different were also providing her with a refuge from being sociable.

We all have to learn to make friends, to rub along with other people and children have to be helped to think about their part in difficulties with peer relations. But Tara had an obvious and immediate explanation for her difficulties and had not been encouraged to think any further than that the other children were jealous of her "super brain power".

Tara began to find herself in a double bind. She needed adult friendship but, of course, she also desperately wanted to have friends of her own age and to feel she belonged to her peer group. She gradually became contemptuous of her teachers, often describing them (admittedly not in their hearing) as stupid and incompetent. Deep down, gifted children can feel surprisingly humiliated.

Tara was ashamed she had no friends and her mockery of her teachers was her way of living a reversal—she felt humiliated and mocked and set out to pass on the pain by being the humiliator and mocker.

Andrea Clifford-Poston

Impact on adults

Gifted children cross adult/child boundaries. Adults can feel threatened by gifted children, especially children with gifted intelligence. We may feel a sense of awe around a child with a special talent, such as art or music; it seems relatively easy to admire them and to warm to them. Perhaps children like Tara worry us because they risk shaming us. We all live with the fear, conscious or unconscious, of being exposed about something, and above all, adults are supposed to *know* to the extent that it feels as though there is something wrong with *not knowing*. Gifted children can remind us of what we haven't achieved! However gifted the Taras of this world may be, they are, of course, children and they need adults to see them as such.

Tara's playworkers' reaction highlights for us a crucial issue in giftedness—what do adults feel they have to do with the gift? For example, if parents notice their three year old can play Mozart by ear what do they feel the child is demanding? Is the child saying "*I must have first class piano lessons*" or simply "*I love playing the piano?*" The question is what is the child asking for, if anything?

Sometimes a gifted child in the family, school or club may be unconsciously expected to act as a redeemer for the adults. Tara's parents had not had the opportunity to fulfil their own academic potential and they were determined that Tara was going to achieve hers, for both Tara's sake and, in a way, to compensate them. This made it difficult for them to keep a balance between Tara's giftedness and the rest of her personality, causing Tara an additional problem as she approached the pre-teen stage.

She knew her parents valued her academic prowess but she was beginning to turn her interests to more teenage preoccupations. As she lacked the support of a peer group she was more than usually troubled at the idea of upsetting her parents.

Impact on peers

Tara had difficulty in settling in club mainly because of her rather brash attitude towards the other children. Her playworkers tried to help her to understand how the other children construed her behaviour as showing off. They encouraged her to try less forceful ways of expressing her views and answers.

The most powerful influence on the way a group of children treat the gifted child lies in the attitude of the adults around them. Other children will feel envious, they may feel shamed by their lack of ability and they may feel awkward around a child who is different. They will need help to see beyond the gift to the ordinary child, who is likely to be exactly at their level emotionally. You can facilitate this by asking questions like, "*What do you think you have that Tara would like?*" One boy who was envious of his friend who had flown all round the world with his musical gift responded to such a question with a shocked silence and then, "*Well, he never gets to play football with his dad.*"

Managing the gifted child

- Hold in mind the relationship between the gifted child and their needs. It is important to meet their gift *and* their needs.

- Help the child to realise they are more than their gift by valuing other qualities. Tara's playworkers made a point of praising her for ordinary qualities: "*You are a helpful person,*" indicating that she was not just an intelligent person. Don't let the idea that the child is special and different provide them with a way of not thinking about why their friendships are not working and their part in them.

- Avoid the temptation to suggest the gifted child level down or hide their gift to make friends. Help them to understand the impact their gift may have on other children n and help them to work out ways of managing it.

- If other children think things are not fair agree with them! Try to avoid compensatory remarks such as, "*But you are so good at swimming,*" but rather comment "*It is disappointing you are not as clever as Tara, but you have things she would like.*"

PART SIX:
THE FAMILY AND THE
OUTSIDE WORLD

BODY TALK:
CHILDREN AND SEX

After school club children may be
struggling to deal with their emerging
sexuality. How do we respond?

Children today are surrounded by sex. There is no innocence anywhere. The boundary between childhood and
adulthood has become blurred.

Research by Mintel in 2004 showed that most 7–10 year
old girls wore make-up sometimes; 83% used nail polish;
66% used lipstick. The research also revealed that girls
as young as seven were deciding on whether to pursue
education, or a boyfriend. Club aged children are being
researched and targeted by manufacturers enticing them
into the pseudo-mature world of discos, make-up and
sexually provocative clothing.

"Sex just wasn't on our agenda at that age," explained
one worried worker. But we are all born with "sex on the
agenda". Sexuality begins with curiosity about our own
bodies and our parents' bodies. Babies explore both by
sucking, touching, gazing. Small children become preoccupied with their bodies—what goes on inside them and
what comes out of them.

You remember the "lavatorial" stage when children
around four or five find it highly amusing to use "rude"
words in public. They collapse into hysterical giggles as they
repeat words like "bum" or "pooh" at any given opportunity. This age group are becoming aware of the differences
between boys and girls. They explore their curiosity through
games of mummies and daddies, doctors and nurses.

Sometimes adults may be embarrassed or shocked by these games, knowing that behind the game the child is wondering about the adult world of "where do babies come from?"

This intense period of curiosity is followed by latency, the time from seven to nine when sexual curiosity is less obvious and displaced into playing games, mainly with children of the same sex, and also into education and learning.

So it can be a shock for workers when little bits and pieces of sexual knowledge or curiosity begin to appear in club through dress, behaviour or language. We may feel things are getting out of control. And part of our anxiety is based on fact: these children are learning the facts of life in school and may also have begun puberty, so they are curious about the relationship between their knowledge and experience. The worry for adults is that nowadays at age eleven or twelve many children are physically able to become parents.

Whose problem is it?

We need to bear in mind that club aged children are not teenagers ready (and eager!) to experiment with sexual experiences. They are much more interested in their own bodies than anyone else's. They want to learn *about sex*, particularly the romantic element of sex. They may spend hours talking about what sex might be like, or about "who's snogging who," but when it comes to themselves, as one eleven year old girl said: "*No lip stuff and absolutely no tongue stuff.*"

They may be poring over magazines, appear fascinated with storylines in soaps and ask to watch over-age movies, but these activities seem to be much more as a way of learning about sex than engaging in it.

They may be preoccupied with the fact that their nose is too big, their eyes too small, the size of their penis or breasts and the small birthmark on their left arm which is sure to prevent anyone from wanting to date them!

Most of all, they want their peers to see them as "cool." In this sense, they are wondering how likely they are to find a sexual partner. Their bedrooms may be plastered with posters of pop stars, film stars or soap stars. They may spend hours in discussion over who is "hot" and who is not, and are likely to be fantasising about having a relationship, or even just raw sex, with their chosen idol. Some may have boy/girl relationships involving kissing but, as I have written elsewhere (Clifford-Poston, 2005) even these relationships are highly likely to be as described by one mother: "*She is more of a girl-boy than a girlfriend, they spend their time on the computer together.*"

In the chapter on "betweenagers" we were thinking about how club aged children are rehearsing what it will be like to be a teenager, they are if you like "playing at it." What they want adults to do is to watch the play, to take it seriously, but to know it is a play! If we respond to them as though they are wanting to have sex, then we miss the essence of their struggle and can actually cause problems by increasing their anxiety.

What this age group needs is:

- To understand how the physical changes in their bodies are impacting on their feelings and behaviour.
- To understand why they feel so uncomfortable in their changing bodies.

179

- To understand how they are going to be able to feel as comfortable as is possible with their emerging sexuality.

They need help to manage these in an age-appropriate way. While they need to know the basic facts of life, more importantly, they need help to understand when sexual intimacy is and is not appropriate within a relationship. The better a youngster's self-esteem, the easier it is for them to say "no". What they need most is enough self-esteem to find out, at their own pace and in their own time, what they want sexually and how to go about getting it.

Helping children with sex

Children's sexual development is as individual and idiosyncratic as a fingerprint. We also have to accept that no one is an expert on sex. We need to move away from the idea that there is "a right age" for talking to children about sexual matters. It is much more important to recognise when a child is ready, by observing subtle changes in the way you react to them.

For example, one holiday club had held a sleepover for two years running. Several staff members felt uncomfortable about running it for the third year. They were unsure why but kept saying they had anxieties about "policing the twelve year olds". This seemed to be an indication that they were aware of a new stage of development for these children.

Whilst we can understand their anxieties, we need to understand these youngsters' communications about sex are less about wanting to lose their virginity and more about whether or not they "look cool." And "looking cool" is their way of telling us that they are concerned about how they are going to cope in the world outside the familiar security of home. This is very different to teenagers who may be preoccupied with *how* they are going to leave home. Play-workers can perform such an important role in helping children to feel confident and admired in the world of club, which in a sense is a transition between home and school and the outside world.

- Build up self-esteem by complimenting youngsters more on some aspect of their personality or behaviour than appearance.
- Don't argue when they complain that they are unattractive! Sympathising, by saying something like *"Yes, I can see you are very disappointed to have brown hair instead of blonde."* may be more of an invitation for the youngster to talk about how they feel about themselves than persuading them that although they haven't got blonde hair, they have got very pretty eyes, etc.
- Storylines from soaps, films or news items are a help-ful way of discussing sexual matters indirectly. For example, many playworkers have had useful conversa-tions about teenage pregnancy by ostensibly sharing views and opinions on a teenage pregnancy storyline in the soap *Neighbours!*

When should we be worried?

Children are now exposed to so much sexual material through the media that we cannot always presume that any worrying behaviour results from what they have experienced rather than from what they might have seen. Whilst it is important to stay alert to indications that a child may be in trouble, don't jump to the sole conclusion of sexual abuse. There are two important signs to keep in mind:

1—Excessive telling of dirty jokes

One of the ways children of this age explore and try to understand sex is by telling dirty jokes. Often it is obvious they don't understand the joke themselves, or are trying to shock. However, when a youngster constantly tells crude sexual jokes and goes on telling them even when they have been asked not to, then you should be alert to the possibility of sexual abuse.

2—Explicit sexual behaviour

Any explicit sexual behaviour from a club aged child should be taken seriously. This is not normally an age for experimenting, it is an age of "curiosity". An eight year old who had been behaving in a sexually explicit way in club was found to have seen an adult ("blue") movie late at night without his parents' knowledge. He had been disturbed by the images and his behaviour was a way of playing them out, trying to make sense of them.

So while this kind of behaviour doesn't necessarily mean a child has been abused, it does mean that there is something about sex which is seriously worrying them and with which they need the attention and understanding of an adult.

SEPARATE WAYS: HELPING CHILDREN WITH DIVORCE

Playworkers are likely to become involved in children's reactions when their parents are divorcing

Nearly half of all children in this country will experience their parents getting divorced (Royal College of Psychiatrists, 2004). Single and reconstituted families are so much a part of society it is easy to forget the impact that divorce can have on children. The lack of social stigma in the outside world may enhance our complacency but in their own internal world a child may feel shamed, guilty, distressed and anxious.

There are, of course, as many ways of children reacting to their parents' divorce as there are children. Adults should not jump to conclusions about how a child may react, but we also need to hold in mind that divorce can have a powerful effect on a child.

Much will depend on how parents manage the issue themselves. There is all the difference in the world between warring parents who constantly denigrate each other in an attempt to get the child to take their side, and parents who work hard to try to remain a united parental couple, putting the children's needs first and trying hard not to overexpose their differences or hostilities to the children. It will also depend on how simple, honest and age appropriate facts and explanations are given to the child.

All change

There are an array of ways families will deal with this change over time; as professionals working with children, we need to be aware that divorce is an unpredictable business. We also need to keep in mind that for a child there is no good enough reason why their parents should separate.

At an emotional level, parents and children share the powerful experience of accepting that their lives have changed for ever. Children, sometimes suddenly, will be faced with saying goodbye to their current way of living; and goodbye makes us sad and angry! So the first task for adults, be it parents or professionals, is to help the children to accept that their parents have separated—but also to help them to try to make the best of the situation—as much as they can—so it doesn't spoil everything else in their lives.

Adults can tend to go to extremes over children's reactions; tending to either presume that their whole world has been completely shattered or to believe that they are relatively unaffected. It can be just as unhelpful to presume that every change in the child's behaviour is due to the divorce as it is to assert boldly that the children are unaffected or even much happier. Of course, there are extremes in children's behaviour too—some children may be traumatised, while others may seem more content because they are not living in a war zone.

Complex reactions

It is important to remember children process life events at their own pace and in their own time. Some children will react instantly, others may seem to take divorce in their stride, sometimes for a long time before another incident triggers a crisis.

Eight year old Jake's parents had divorced when he was four years old, since when he had gradually lost touch with his father. He had been attending after school club since he began school. John had been a constant staff member during this time and Jake became distraught when John announced he was leaving his job. Jake was inconsolable for weeks, crying, "*I'll never see him again, I'll never see him again.*"

Jake was clearly fond of John and had a good relationship with him; what became clear was that by saying goodbye John had reawakened Jake's distress at saying goodbye to his father; he was now able to express his sadness for the first time. So it is important in child care to take the long term view and to be aware of a delayed reaction from a child.

Children between four and seven years old still tend to see themselves as the centre of their world and presume they are the cause or effect of all their life events. When asked why he thought his father had left, Jake replied, "*I don't know, but I think I was naughty.*" This reply came in spite of the fact that he had been given age-appropriate facts at the time. Children who feel they are the cause for the divorce may try very hard to be "good" and not show their true feelings for fear of causing more trouble. Such children may become quiet and withdrawn, sleeping and eating poorly, and their school work may suffer. Sometimes they may resort to petty pilfering or even stealing as a concrete way of showing that they feel they have been robbed of something emotional and they want to steal it back.

185

Such children may become cautious in relationships with adults, often seeming to be scanning adults' faces constantly in an attempt to read their mood or behaviour. This was highlighted to one playworker after she returned to club having missed three sessions due to illness. As she entered the room, she saw seven year old Daisy's face light up. Daisy began to rush towards her and then stopped in her tracks looking shy and uncertain; she then stood still in an almost ashamed manner until the playworker approached her.

Older children in club may feel more angry than sad. They live in a world of comparisons—who has what, who can do what, who has the best, who has the most. Eleven year old Martin didn't want to attend holiday club the year his parents separated. "*It's so not fair,*" he raged, "*I don't want people to know my home is split up . . . it's so not fair.*" Such children may experience their share of guilt and sadness but most of all they are likely to feel that they have been singled out for a raw deal. You may find them in an almost permanent state of outrage, everything may be "so not fair." As Martin's playworker said, "*If I choose him to do something I'm picking on him, if I don't choose him it's because I don't like him!*"

We need to be especially alert to families where one child seems unable to come to terms with their parents' divorce but their siblings seem to be coping well with their new life.

We have already thought about how children take on different roles in the family. Sometimes, such a child may be working very hard on behalf of their siblings by taking on the role of "the unhappy one," i.e., carrying all the pain and distress, leaving the other children free to get on with their lives. Such families may need professional help to redress the balance of distress in the family.

Supporting children

Children need facts in order to make sense of emotional situations. Paradoxically, in emotional situations, there are no absolute facts! Most importantly children need to be reassured that divorce is "adult business" and that nothing they can have said or done would cause their parents to separate.

If you are concerned about a child it is important to share your concerns with the parents. In doing so, you will need to remember it is almost impossible to give parents any support in helping their child without increasing their guilt and anxiety about the children. It is almost impossible not to imply that it was not in the children's best interests for them to separate! Try to find out how the parents are coping both with themselves and the children and whether or not they need and would like some professional help.

In divorce, families have to find out how they want to be together and the ways in which this can be managed. Sometimes you can help by making a life-book with the child, telling the story of their life up to the divorce: what they did and didn't enjoy doing with their parents until then. Then get them to draw or imagine the story of their future life with their parents. This can be painful, for it seems as though all children, however old they are, harbour the desire that their parents will one day get back together. You can explain to the child that there is nothing wrong with wanting and wishing this but that it is not going to happen. It is important that such a longing does not become a life preoccupation for a child.

Allow the child to feel whatever they are feeling. This may seem obvious but adults can be overwhelmed in the face of children's sadness and distress. We can make tremendous efforts to distract them or cheer them up. It is very important that children are allowed to express exactly how it feels for them and to have those feelings heard and understood. If a child feels that what is real to them is real to you, then they are linked to life, the world and meaningful relationships.

UNITED AND DIVIDED: RECONSTITUTED FAMILIES

Children struggling with
upheaval at home as their parents
settle in with new partners may take
out their feelings in your club

When parents separate, something that everyone took for granted and thought would be permanent has turned out not to be so. Children may feel their firm foundation has turned to sand, leaving them bewildered and disorientated. The main task for parents and care workers alike is to help children to accept the separation and to make the best they can of it.

Writing in the 1960s, Mary Ainsworth talked of children's need for "a secure base" from which they could explore the world intellectually, physically and emotionally (see Ainsworth and Wittig, 1969). Traditionally this secure base was provided by two parents who love each other and who love the child. But nowadays in club you see all kinds of families—single parent families, same-sex parent families, and reconstituted families.

The relative success of some of these families gives us hope. I have written elsewhere (Clifford-Poston, 2007) how marriage does not necessarily equate with "family" or "home". These are three separate ideas which may often overlap and co-exist but which are able to operate independently as well. And none of us choose our parents: we all take what we get and make the best of it.

Children's reactions to remarriage

"Will you still be my mummy?" asked an anxious seven year old Tamsin when her mother told her that she was going to remarry. Tamsin lived with her father but spent one week day night and every other weekend with her mother. It wasn't that she didn't like her future stepfather, but more that like many children of divorced parents, she had always hoped that one day her parents would be reunited. For some children such a hope can almost become a purpose for living. Tamsin was suddenly realising for the first time that "divorce" meant that her parents were never going to live together again.

Tamsin highlights how remarriage is very much a choice made by adults and foisted onto children. Parents may well take their children's feelings into consideration with regard to timing and manner of a remarriage, but children cannot choose if, whom or when their parents may find a new partner.

Much will depend on an individual child's personality, age and needs, and also on the level of disruption in the child's life. Have they had to move house, schools, even the area in which they live? Is the reconstituted family going to live in a totally new house for everyone, or is one set of children going to have join another set in their family home? Perhaps the biggest influencing factor is the relationship between the separated parents. If parents can manage to remain a parental couple, as opposed to a sexual couple, and are able to be amicable in front of the children, then children are likely to be able to have a sense of their parents "together" in their minds. If separated parents can manage to keep the child in "a secure base"—that is, not tear them apart emotionally—many children seem to negotiate this process relatively smoothly.

However, we all know that reconstituted families differ from biological families. First and foremost, everyone in the family is not related by blood and this is bound to colour the adults' attitude to the way the children are parented. However outrageously a child behaves in a biological family, and however much the parents may disagree on management, they are parenting with the same instinctive desire to protect this person who is part of themselves.

A step-parent may not necessarily share this instinct. They may feel full of goodwill towards their partner's children and do their very best to create a loving relationship with them. However, they may also find themselves feeling angry, resentful and jealous towards them.

"I find it so hard to tolerate the love in her eyes when he comes into the room," said one step-father of his wife's relationship with her son. A step-child not only enjoys a special relationship with the blood parent, they are a constant reminder of the previous relationship. They may also upset and hurt their step-siblings.

Parenting in a reconstituted family is complex and complicated by strong feelings. The ongoing task of each family is to discover how they are going to unite all these disparate relationships and ensure a degree of harmony in the family. A key part in this struggle for harmony is to remember that all families run into problems along the way, and this is as unavoidable as it is natural. Even when a good step-parent is creating a much happier home than the family they have had previously, there are bound to be hiccups and traumas.

It is probably true that all families are founded on an unrealistic sense of idealism and optimism. How much more is that true of the reconstituted family—the adults will be rejoicing at the opportunity of a second chance of happiness. At an unconscious level, they may also be hoping that this new family will redeem their earlier unhappiness, so parents may enter a reconstituted family expecting it to be far more perfect than is ever possible. They may also fall into the trap of believing that both sets of children are sharing their joy and optimism. Of course, this may or may not be true.

Children may be dealing with painful and conflicting feelings that they can't put into words. Children are intrinsically loyal to their own parents, and it is common for step-children to feel that they are betraying their natural parent if they become fond of the step-parent. So children need time and space to develop relationships within the reconstituted family.

Struggling to cope with identity— "Who am I in this new family?"

Children may have lost daily contact, sometimes all contact, with one parent. They may also have lost their position in the family. An interesting situation arose in club one day with nine year old Jordan. He had been the club captain for a term and was now being asked to step down to number two to give another child the opportunity. Jordan knew this was the way that the captaincy operated in his club but his play leaders were astonished at his reaction as he handed over his badge.

As he threw it at his successor he shouted *"Oh go on— I'm number two now!"*

Jordan had been an only child, but when his mother remarried in the school holidays he gained an older brother and a younger sister. He felt threatened and displaced by the change from being the first and only child to being "second son" and this had spilled over into club life.

Increasing competitive behaviour

Orly had become increasingly competitive in after school club. She found it difficult to share, always wanted to win, and would become very distressed when she lost. She had always been a child who needed a lot of adult attention, more than one might expect from a ten year old, but this had escalated to a worrying degree since her mother's re-marriage. Orly had moved from being one of two children to being one of four in the family. She felt she had to compete twice as hard now for her mother's time, love and attention.

Aggressive behaviour

Rex, on the other hand, had become increasingly aggressive and resentful in club. He picked fights with the other children and was surly and defiant with staff, particularly female staff. Things came to head one day when his play worker intervened in a squabble for the third time, saying "*Rex, I've told you three times . . .*"

Rex spun round on her. "*You're not my mum, you can't tell me anything!*" he shouted in rage.

Rex was displacing his resentment of his step-mother and siblings onto the children and playworkers at club.

Rex needed to be able to feel what he was feeling—sad, jealous and angry. He needed time and space to understand how he felt. His playworkers helped him by giving him names for his feelings—for example, "*Lots of nine year olds have secret feelings about their step-siblings, some feel very jealous.*" They helped him to understand how he was confusing club and home and encouraged him to talk to his father about how he felt. Sometimes children are so overwhelmed by their strong feelings they need help to think about them rather than act them out.

Insecure and anxious behaviour

Quiet and withdrawn, eight year old Lily was becoming increasingly solitary in club. Her playworkers worried as they noticed her on the fringe of groups, hanging back as though she didn't know how to join in. When encouraged to do so, she would say, "*Well, I'm not sure . . . I'm just not sure,*" seeming unsure of exactly what it was she was unsure about.

It can be painful for adults to tolerate the ambiguity and uncertainty involved in change. Not surprisingly, children can find it traumatic. Like unsure Lily, they may act out what they are feeling, often regressing to an earlier stage of development. Lily had been the baby until her three year old step-sister joined them. Her playworkers were not surprised to hear that she had recently had episodes of bedwetting.

How club can help

One of the tasks of a reconstituted family is to accept that they are not a nuclear family. Parenting is going to be interrupted daily by family life. Family members have to accept that changes are necessary for the family to live in a healthy and happy way. They have to begin to work together to create new family rules, rituals and boundaries.

Playworkers can be an enormous resource for parents at such a time, having as you do daily contact with the children in a setting which in many ways mirrors family life.

However, you must bear in mind that it is very difficult to help parents in a reconstituted family without making them feel guilty about the original divorce and separation.

Lily's parents were initially angry with the playworkers and blamed them for Lily's difficulties. They felt it was the playworkers' job to make it easy for Lily to mix with other children. It is painful for parents to witness their children's unhappiness, and you may have to accept that parents won't always seem grateful for your help.

And finally, what about club—what do reconstituted families say about club? It is always worth thinking about what kind of "parent" your club is. How do staff behave towards staff? How do children behave towards children? What spirit of relationship is fostered? The best way for children to learn how to be flexible, how to compromise, and how to understand their own and other people's viewpoints, is to have flexibility, compromise and understanding modelled by the adults surrounding them.

HEADLINE NEWS: MANAGING NATIONAL AND WORLD TRAUMA

Media coverage of wars and disasters means playworkers will need to respond to children's anxieties and their questions

One of the biggest differences between our lives and the lives of previous generations is that now so much more is witnessed through a camera lens. National and world tragedies are brought into our living rooms as they happen.

In the past, bad news (and certainly its accompanying photographs) took time to travel, and the people involved may well have begun to recover before the news broke in another country. Now raw war is seen in action and children witness events such as soldiers storming buildings and taking—and even killing—prisoners, as they occur. In this sense, war has become entertainment, and it is the same with natural disasters and acts of terrorism.

And the media is driven to bring us the "whole story." Traumatised family members are interviewed in states of shock, anger and complete devastation, often sobbing out their stories while we are shown close-ups of homes, bouquets of flowers, and wreaths, with the camera zooming in on the most touching of tributes.

Real life trauma

Children today watch more television than any previous generation, and many watch in their bedrooms without adult supervision. So, children are often watching real-life trauma long before they are able to distinguish fact from fiction.

Most stories for children feature distress, pain and conflict as the main character endures a period of suffering and abuse before they achieve their goal. Children can cope with such themes providing the endings are not falsely reassuring or depressing; children need endings they can use and that work for them. I remember reading *I Am David* to a class of ten year olds and an audible sigh was breathed round the room as I read the last line indicating that David had reached the end of his journey happily.

Wars, terrorism and natural disasters rarely have fairy-tale endings, and often have endings which are distressing for us all. So what do we tell the children and how much do we tell them? To what extent should we be raising their awareness of world events and to what extent should we try and sanitise them?

Younger club aged children will still be living in a fairly egocentric world, meaning they are more concerned with what affects them and their lives directly. Following the floods in Boscastle in August 2004, we can understand the seven year old in Cornwall who was found stacking his pillows against his bedroom door in case ". . . *the floods come up here.*" We are also not surprised that children in other parts of the country may not have attached much relevance to this natural disaster.

Older children tend to absorb not only what is relevant to them, but also what they are ready to learn and, like the younger child, may well dismiss the rest.

If a child asks questions about national and world events, we can assume that they want to be told something about them. What we cannot presume is exactly what it is they are questioning. For example, if a child asks why the Palestinians hate the Israelis, they may be asking for a factual answer about the problems in the Middle East. However, they may also be asking about hating—why one feels hate and how one manages hatred. Children often use questions about the external world as a way of making sense of their feelings.

Age and experience

Children need to be given information which is both appropriate for their age and for their life experience. Let us think about an incident discussed in a support group for club leaders working in an area where many of the children in club had parents in the army. They had noticed that the children seemed to take the idea of a parent being posted to Iraq in their stride: this was their parent's job. While some spoke openly about missing their parents, they did so in the context of any child missing an absent parent. None expressed fears about their parent's safety and many seemed proud of the work their parents were doing.

However, the club leaders did notice that some of these children seemed more boisterous and played more aggressive games than previously. They wondered if this was the way the children were both expressing their own anxieties and also trying to play out what might be happening to their parents.

When the first British soldiers were killed in action pictures of the solemn, ceremonial return of their bodies were shown on the television. The next day eight year old Sam was particularly quiet and withdrawn in club until his play leader found him sitting at a table, his face cupped in his hands as he stared gloomily into space. As she sat down next to him, two tears rolled silently down his cheeks and he whispered "*Will my daddy be killed?*"

What is the most helpful way for this play leader to respond? Some members of the group felt she should reassure the child his father would return safe and well, especially as statistically this was the most likely scenario. Others felt an honest "*I don't know but I hope not*" was the best answer, as this was the truth. Everybody felt the question would be easier to answer if posed by a non-army child as reported by another club leader. An eight year old in her group had asked the same question after a news item reported a policeman shot on duty. This child was particularly affected by seeing the policeman's son who was the same age as him. Here it was felt easier to say something like "*Your daddy is not a policeman and so it is very unlikely.*" However, it may also be important to help the child to be realistic by adding something like "*Of course, we will all die some day, but hopefully this won't be for a very long time and not until you are really quite grown up.*"

For Sam, realism had to be modified to a digestible version such as "*Some soldiers do get killed in wars but hopefully your daddy will live for a long, long time yet.*"

Asking questions

When children ask questions, it is always worth wondering if the child is speaking on behalf of someone else. In any major crisis, children's attitudes and behaviour are most coloured by the way the adults around them behave and manage their feelings about what is happening. Sam was voicing his own worry, but he was also undoubtedly voicing his mother's worry.

Children are acutely sensitive to adults' emotional states at the best of times. In the worst of times, they turn to adults to help them make sense of their fears and worries. And when it comes to national and world disasters, terrorism, and wars this gives us a problem, for we are often put in the position of trying to explain to children events—like tsunami, or famine—which we cannot begin to comprehend ourselves. Our bewilderment adds to our distress, which children are almost bound to sense. It is frightening for a child to feel that the adults on whom they rely for comfort are themselves distressed and unable to cope.

A play leader recently told how she opened a newspaper in front of some children in club to be faced with the most moving pictures of families starving in Uganda. She found her eyes filling with tears and was aware the group around her had quietened and were watching her with an expression of slight panic.

Perhaps the most helpful way of managing such a situation is to be unafraid to show your sadness, but also to show how you can manage it with something like " *These pictures make me so sad I want to* cry . . . *It's alright to be sad . . . but maybe we had better get on with what we are doing now.* " This may give the children a chance to say anything they want or need to say concerning the pictures, but it also conveys that it is not their responsibility to comfort you. Dismissing your tears, or ignoring the response of the children, may give the impression there is something so worrying that it can't be talked about, or that you cannot focus on them.

Positive acts

From about eight years onward, children begin to develop a strong sense of justice and fair play. As they begin to take more interest in the world outside home, they can be real motivators for change in the community. They can have a very prosaic, focussed reaction to tragedies and disasters by believing that they can solve the problem by raising money for aid through baking and selling biscuits, sponsored events, and little jumble sales, etc.

In her book *Love, Hate and Reparation*, Melanie Klein talks about how we are all frightened of our own aggression and seek to make reparation for it. We can think of these children as unconsciously trying to make something good on behalf of the adults. They may not only increase adults' awareness of world events, they can even shame us into raising or giving money ourselves. They certainly convey to the community as a whole that something can be done in the face of seemingly overwhelming and impossible situations.

MEET THE PARENTS:
WORKING WITH FAMILIES

Have you ever been on the receiving
end of an angry parent's wrath and
needed help to diffuse the situation?
This chapter explores ways for
playworkers to develop good
relationships

Play leaders and parents both want children to enjoy club
as much as possible. In this sense, they are always working
together, so it is interesting that talking to each other can
be potentially fraught with difficulty.

When children, parents and staff come to club, they
bring much more than the obvious. All three come with
conscious, or thought about, expectations. They also
bring unconscious, or not thought about, expectations. And
it is these unconscious expectations that can muddle
conversations.

Let us think about eight year old Stephanie at after school
club. One evening Stephanie got into a scuffle and received
a small scratch on her face. Her play leader, Margaret, was
quick on the scene. She assessed the situation as a "six-of-
one and half-a-dozen of the other" kind. As the scratch was
slight and superficial, she took no further action.

Stephanie continued to attend club happily. However,
a couple of weeks later, the club leader heard that
Stephanie's father had complained to his MP that his
daughter had been bullied in club, the staff had taken no
action, and he "*wanted something done*".

Margaret was angry and indignant. She felt she had managed the situation appropriately and the criticism of her was unfair. She had always experienced Stephanie as a slightly sly child, who was inevitably somewhere in the middle of any explosive situation, and Margaret now told the club leader that she didn't want to work with Stephanie any more. The club leader was also annoyed that Stephanie's father had not discussed the incident with her or Margaret, but had gone over her head. She intended to support Margaret, who was young and inexperienced, but good at her job.

What play leaders bring to club

Anyone would have been irritated at the way this father had behaved. However, as play leaders you bring to club your skills, your training, an interest in children, and the desire to do your job well, and you also bring your own childhood experiences.

How you approach parents is coloured by how your parents behaved towards you. When parents and play leaders talk, at one level two adults are talking. At another, play leaders are going to experience parents as they experienced their own parents. So if, as a child, Margaret's parents had helped and encouraged her when she got things wrong, she would be likely to approach this father confidently, believing that this situation could be resolved. If, on the other hand, her parents had viewed "getting it wrong" as failure, then Margaret may well approach the father feeling defensive, and possibly, aggressive.

You also bring to club your expectations about how you will do your job. If you expect you have to do your job perfectly, rather than "well enough", then talking to parents may place you in a double bind. Margaret could feel that if she had been doing her job perfectly the scuffle would not have happened in the first place. She is then faced with having to explain to Stephanie's father that she believes she handled the situation appropriately, whilst at the same time, believing it was her fault.

What parents bring to club

- The expectation that their child will be cared for by appropriately trained adults.
- The expectation that their child will be happy at club.
- Their own view of themselves as a parent—do they believe they are the expert on their child or do they believe you are the expert on their child? Or do they believe there is an expertise that can be shared between the two of you?
- Their own childhood experiences of authority figures.

The club leader asked Stephanie's father to meet her. He was initially belligerent, insisting *"I was bullied as a kid, and no one is going to bully my kid."*

Parents bring to club their own childhood experiences. They will always crusade at the club gates against what they found most difficult as a child. Stephanie's father was determined she was not going to be bullied as he had been.

As the conversation continued, Stephanie's father refused to believe his daughter's part in the scuffle. He denied she might have been aggressive in this incident, insisting *"I know my daughter best,"* and demanding, *"I want something done . . ."* He had learned by the way his teachers had treated him that professionals can misconstrue children—his teachers had ignored his complaints and so he grew up feeling authority figures didn't listen. He was so sensitive to the risk of Stephanie being bullied that he presumed it, even when it wasn't happening. He felt the play leaders wouldn't listen, as his teachers hadn't listened; he distrusted the play leader's view of his daughter, and so he had gone to the top by contacting his MP.

Accept how parents feel

"*What would you like done?*" asked the club leader quietly. The situation was diffused as the father suddenly fell silent. Parents may be overwhelmed by a desire to protect their child—so overwhelmed that they may not have thought about what they want done before complaining. An apology? An expulsion? A play leader sacked? What? Finding out what will satisfy the parent may have a two-fold result: firstly, it may make the parent stop and think, and secondly, it may form a basis for discussion.

Put simply, complaining parents often want to vent feelings. The risk is that you may respond logically with the facts of the situation, and the parent may then feel unheard. Saying something like, "*I can understand you are very angry and what would you like done?*" may help the parent to feel heard and so to think further.

It is interesting how "and" is so much more constructive than "but"! The risk of saying "... **but what do you want done?**" is that the parent will only hear the "but" and think you are disagreeing with them! "And" seems to bring people closer together, "but" seems to create distance between people.

Helping parents to hear

Playworkers are often in the delicate position of having to talk to parents about a child's worrying or disruptive behaviour. Stephanie had been as much the aggressor as the victim in this incident, but how could the club leader help her father to think about his daughter's behaviour? If you criticise a child to its parents, you run the risk that the parent will feel you are criticising their parenting. Any parent will want to defend their offspring, and themselves, against criticism. A conversation of persuasion is likely to ensue, with the parent trying to persuade you to their viewpoint—and conversely, you trying to persuade the parent to yours!

You are likely to get much further with a parent by saying something like "*We are a bit worried about Tom at club; how has he been at home lately?*" than, for example, "*Tom is being aggressive in club*".

If you want to get parents on your side, then you will have to allow them to disagree with you. After all, there is no reason why anyone should agree with anybody else about anything! Saying something like "*Well, we don't have to agree about this . . . and we are very concerned about Tom at club. Maybe he is different at home. Do you know if he has any worries at club?*" may help to keep the conversation going, and the parent to feel you are on their side.

When parents feel guilty

Some parents may bring a further "not thought about" expectation to club—the expectation that good parents don't send their children to clubs. Some children attend club by choice, seeing it as a fun step to independence. Others have to attend because parents are working. The children's view of club will be coloured by the reason they attend, and so will their parents' view. Some parents may feel very guilty, and therefore sensitive to comments made by playworkers. It is easy to increase a sense of failure in such a parent, particularly if their child has developed problems at club.

The best way to get parents on your side is to make them feel that you are on their side. It is important to start the conversation with where the parents are, be it belligerent or co-operative. Sometimes you may have to be a "double agent", sympathising with both the parents' and the child's viewpoint.

Talking to parents needs skill, sensitivity, warmth, and a dose of charm. It is not a competition over who knows best for a child, but rather an attempt to return to your original position of both working together to ensure that a child enjoys their time at club.

Getting Parents on Your Side

- Start where the parents are.
- Accept how the parents feel.
- Allow parents to disagree with you.
- Avoid criticism.
- Avoid conversations of persuasion.
- Try to use "and" instead of "but".
- Make parents feel you are on their side.

MOVING ON: HELPING CHILDREN WITH THE TRANSFER TO SECONDARY SCHOOL

Children know transition from primary to secondary school is an enormous event in their lives, but don't presume they understand what is happening

"It's always the same at this time of year. All of our Year 6 kids start getting twitchy—they are either hyper or irritable, or just plain sulky. They just get too big for their boots, we are glad to see them go in a way," sighed an after school club leader as she watched a quarrel develop in a group at the corner of the room. Certainly the large group of eleven year olds seemed to be working hard to make their presence felt throughout the session.

Of course, Year 6 children have always known they would move up to secondary school, but as their final summer term in primary school begins, this transition may become both an exciting and a worrying reality. Consciously or unconsciously, they will be thinking about how they will cope in this relatively much larger and more independent world.

Earlier in the book, we thought about how after school club symbolises a step into the world outside home and school, so it is not surprising that many eleven year olds act out their excitement and anxiety in club. Children will choose a variety of ways of showing they may be worried.

Some indeed do become "too big for their boots", using bravado as a way of hiding their fears about being small and not knowing. Others may become withdrawn and uncooperative, almost as though they are trying to freeze themselves in a state of childhood. And, of course, tensions will lead to quarrels and spats between the youngsters.

What transitions mean

From birth to weaning, to walking, to going to school, childhood is full of transitional stages. How a child reacts to a transition tells us a lot about how the child feels about their own development. Transitions reveal a lot about a child's character.

Marie was looking forward to the change. *"It's a bit scary,"* she said, but she was ready for the *"more grown up things; like I can go on the bus by myself, and learn foreign languages and go on trips."*

Marie was admitting some anxieties, but was clearly ready and confident in her skills to cope with this next stage of growing up.

Winston, on the other hand, was fearful. He was worried about almost every aspect of the change. He had to catch the school bus and was *". . . afraid I might miss it, and then you get detention."* He was worried about the size of the building, having to find different classrooms for each lesson, *"What if I get lost, and then you are well in trouble."* He feared the work would be *"Too hard,"* the homework *"too much,"* and he would be bullied by the older boys.

Winston's playworkers were surprised at his reaction as he was not a particularly timid or withdrawn child generally. But he was immature, both physically and emotionally, looking young for his age. He was taking growing up at a slower pace than other children. The move up to secondary school felt like *"A violent catapult"* to him.

Each transitional stage in growing up will remind a child of their early experiences and all transitions are prepared for with echoes of previous ones.

Marie and Winston both remembered their first day at primary school. Marie had moved naturally from part time nursery to the local school with most of her friends. In the last month of the summer term she had spent one day a week at her new school, and got to know her teacher. Winston had been less fortunate: his family had moved house during the summer holidays and so he had no preparatory visits to his new school. He had no friends to go with him and he felt even more different when his teacher found it difficult to understand his broad Scottish accent.

Learning about differences

Winston's story shows us how painful it can be for a child to feel different. This is an important issue in moving on to secondary school.

Year 5 and 6 children are becoming acutely aware of differences. They are not only learning new facts, views and opinions, they are also discovering how social differences—such as family income—can affect them, which may be illustrated by their becoming aware of the two kinds of school on offer: the state system and the private system.

But, of course, one of the biggest differences Year 6 children are facing is the fact that they will have been seniors in their primary school, and in club some will have had positions of responsibility, such as being a prefect. At the senior school they are going to be the most junior pupils and the older adolescents will seem much bigger and wiser. They may feel like a "nobody" but the exciting aspect is that they have a new set of people to emulate and hero-worship.

The other central difference to the life of children of this age is that their bodies are becoming different. They may be feeling more moody, clumsy and self-conscious. All this, just at the time that they are going to have to negotiate making new friends and, possibly, in a much wider social circle. Differences such as these all tap into the serious question a Year 6 child is beginning to ask themselves, *"Where do I fit in?"*

Parents are moving up too

It is not uncommon for club workers to notice a change at this stage, not only in children's behaviour, but also in parents' behaviour. Their child's transition to secondary school is a huge step in a parent's life. It symbolises their child's increasing need for a private life and independence.

Marie's mother had always been supportive and appreciative of the club workers. However, during the summer term she became increasingly irritable with them, constantly checking rules and regulations and Marie's safety. *"She's like a lioness with a little cub—what's happened to her?"* said Marie's key worker wearily.

Parents know that once a child goes to secondary school they are going to be exposed to a whole range of new experiences and opinions, not only those of new teachers and new classmates, but also of the state, and world politics.

211

The change in Marie's mother's behaviour highlights for us how parents may begin to feel panicky about their diminishing influence over their child. They may become overprotective and critical of the other adults caring for their offspring.

How out-of-school clubs can help children with moving on to secondary school

Throughout this book, I have tried to highlight the important opportunities provided by the informal atmosphere of club for therapeutic conversations with children.

Some children will find it difficult to admit to their worries for fear of being seen as babyish or, as one eleven year old commented, *"Well wuss."* But children are much less guarded when playing in club than in other peer settings and playworkers have an opportunity to raise the topic casually.

If you ask whether or not they are looking forward to secondary school you may get the answer they think they ought to give rather than the truth.

Try to keep questions as open as possible, for example, *"How do you think secondary school will be different?"*

- Above all, listen! If they are enthusiastic, join in their excitement. Take their worries seriously. They need to know it is natural to have mixed feelings about any big change in life.
- Be specific in response to their worries. For example, if they are worried about getting lost, talk through with them what they could do if it happened and who they

could approach in their new school if they did have a problem.

- Leaving and preparation ceremonies are crucial and they should be photographed. Children love photographs marking transitions in their lives.
- Some clubs have found it useful to have a formal group "talking time" when Year 6 children can talk quietly with a worker in a corner of the room about what they expect and what they are looking forward to, as well as what they are worrying about in the coming months.

Transitions can make children anxious for many reasons, but not in the least because they may fear what they are leaving is gone forever. It can be reassuring for them to know that you will be pleased to see them if they do want to visit club at any time. This can be particularly supportive if it is presented as how helpful it can be to have Year 7 children talking to Year 6 children about their first year in secondary school.

Most children find the transfer to secondary school a major trauma. They are affected physically and symbolically because they know that an enormous change is happening in their lives. Most will feel they are in the middle of something beyond their control and club workers need to be constantly aware that this is a very powerful experience for both the child and their family.

CONCLUSION: CAN PSYCHOANALYTIC INSIGHT REALLY HELP A CLUB WORKER?

In writing this book it may seem that I am taking for granted that out-of-school club workers' professional skills will be enriched if they understand what a child is communicating by their behaviour. Of course, this is not necessarily so; I do believe our work is enriched by understanding the psychodynamic model of human behaviour. This model emphasises the importance of what goes on unconsciously between people and in groups. When we understand the unconscious motivations that may be at play then our skills in understanding seemingly meaningless behaviour are enhanced.

However, I am also aware that potentially such understanding can complicate a worker's role and give them extra difficulties in their daily work.

In the Introduction I highlighted how a playworker's role is to maintain the group. If we think of children's behaviour as only good or bad, appropriate or inappropriate, then, we can argue, maintaining the group is relatively straightforward. If a child behaves in a way that is unacceptable to the group then they are excluded. However, once we understand that disruptive behaviour can be a child's way of trying to get close to someone in an inappropriate way, then maintaining the group becomes a much more complex task. To exclude such a child may exacerbate their difficulties, and yet the playworker cannot allow the group to be constantly disrupted.

Many out-of-school club workers get scant affirmation for themselves from anybody. The real nature of your achievements is intangible: how can we measure the true success of an out-of-school club worker's work when it involves attempts to sustain relationships with a myriad of children? This lack of external affirmation can make it difficult for playworkers to gain a sense of what they are doing and therefore also find it difficult to value themselves.

One of the risks of a book like this—filled with psychodynamic understanding—is that the club worker may feel more deskilled than skilled after reading it. You may fall into the trap of believing that there is nothing you can do for a child, as everything is predetermined by their experiences of home, especially during the early years. Or, worst of all, there is the risk that you, as a playworker, will be left feeling that your skills are not enough to help a child who clearly needs therapeutic help.

In both these scenarios there is the possibility of you abandoning your skills as an out-of-school club worker. You may feel powerless and that you can do nothing; or you may feel that you have to try to become a quasi-therapist to the child. In a sentence, you may well feel that what you have to offer is not good enough. Nothing could be further from the truth.

I have written elsewhere (Clifford-Poston, 2005) about how punishing children can be a way of not thinking about children. Giving up on your playworker skills may also be a way of not thinking about what you have to offer a child. Feeling deskilled can be a response to understanding how a child feels. Children's feelings are raw and primitive and it is human enough to feel overwhelmed and helpless in the face of them.

Confronted with a disturbed and disturbing child in club, a powerful dynamic can come into play. Many disturbed children feel unwanted, unworthy and rejected. Much of their behaviour is an attempt to test their hypothesis, to ask " have the grown-ups really thrown me out?"

Of course, much of their behaviour *can* lead to them being thrown out of club, but the more interesting fact is the way they can make adults feel unworthy and compelled to look outside for someone with greater skills.

We live in a culture of experts—everyone seems to be seeking advice and enhancement in some area of their life, but nowhere is this more true than in the field of childcare. No one likes to see an unhappy child. Sometimes we process that dislike by believing somewhere there is an expert who has a magic or instant solution for this child.

Experts have their role; an objective eye can often see a meaning in a child's behaviour that has become obscured in the hurly burly of daily club life. However, if you find yourself feeling only an expert can understand a child it is worth giving the matter a little further thought.

- Is this how the child feels: "my pain is so great only a very special person can help?"
- Is there something about the child you find hard to think about and reflect on?
- What are you hoping the expert will do or say?

It is a disappointing fact of life that understanding a problem is not a magic key to solving a problem. There may be no way of solving difficult, disturbing and disruptive behaviour, but rather only ways of working with it. This can be frustrating when one is using all one's resources to try and help a child.

217

We also need to bear in mind that there is a difference between understanding a child and excusing a child for the way they behave. Children can be helped to behave in a more constructive way by making them know that you are trying to understand. However, they also need to be helped to take responsibility for their actions—to own up to their own behaviour and not blame it on someone else, be that another child, staff or their parents.

Children learn how to treat each other by observing and absorbing how the adults around them treat them. Everything you do with one child will register with all the other children in the group. Over-tolerance will have just as much impact on the group as rigid inflexibility.

So what has a book like this got to offer out-of-school club workers? And equally important, what have out-of-school club workers got to offer parents, teachers and other professionals with regard to the management of children?

First of all, we need to make a clear distinction. This book does give specific understanding of and insight into individual children's behaviour. However, its overall message is more about trying to develop a particular way of thinking about children and an overall attitude towards children. If we give children the experience of taking them seriously and trying to understand the reality of the way they experience the world, then we are helping them to take themselves seriously and planting the seeds of the idea that they can think about their worries instead of simply acting them out in worrying behaviour. And we have no idea when in the child's life those seeds may come to fruition.

The two kinds of adults central to a child's world are their parents and their teachers. As I said in the Introduction, out-of-school club workers are neither and so we can think about what not being a child's parent or teacher frees you to do.

Children need to feel contained by adults in any setting they may find themselves. They respond differently to different forms of containment in home, school, and club. The advantage of a club worker's relationship with a child is that club is a brief, less structured, and non-parental contact. Children are free to try things out which they are not free to try out at either home or school. Out-of-school club is a special place for children between home and school. In some ways it is similar to these other places, but also very different. The very naturalness and normality of the out of school club environment makes it the pre-adolescent child's last "experimental" place.

What do I mean by "an experimental place"?

You can help to free children from agendas; many children nowadays are overloaded with agendas. There is the agenda of school where they must succeed. There is the agenda of a plethora of out-of-school activities (it is not uncommon for a child to be doing four or five different activities after school each week). These social activities bring with them the additional agenda of how a child today should look, how they should sound, with whom and how they should socialise. Agendas mould and colour a child's life, but I am not saying this is all bad.

However, what club provides is an opportunity to be spontaneous. The relatively relaxed atmosphere of an out-of-school club frees a child to experiment not only with all kinds of activities and experiences, but also with different versions of themselves. In club children are not having to satisfy parents or teachers. Club workers have a different demand. You provide children with an opportunity to be different from the way they are at home or at school.

219

Many professionals working with children are over-loaded with agendas in their work. This is particularly true of teachers, who nowadays seem governed by targets, tests and the National Curriculum. One of the consequences for such professionals is that in most child organisations, for example schools, we can contain children by organising them.

As an out-of-school club worker, you have the opportunity to offer children a different form of containment. After-school club work is less about organising children and more about looking after children with certain ends in mind. And this may be an important message to professionals in other child settings. As a club worker you have the opportunity to be unlike a parent or teacher and this gives you an interesting and challenging role in the child's life.

While I hope this book will help playworkers (and parents and teachers) to understand the paradox of individual children's behaviour, I hope it will also provide constructive ideas for helping children to understand that their behaviour has to be acceptable to the group if they are to be allowed to remain in club. I also hope this book will heighten all our awareness of the uniqueness and the importance of what playworkers have to offer to our children.

FURTHER READING

Bowlby, J. (1979). *The Making and Breaking of Affectional Bonds.* London: Tavistock Publications.

Clifford-Poston, A. (2005). *Tweens: What to Expect From, and How to Survive, Your Child's Pre-Teenage Years.* Oxford: Oneworld.

Clifford-Poston, A. (2007). *When Harry Hit Sally: Understanding Your Child's Behaviour.* London: Simon & Schuster.

Erikson, E. (1995). *Childhood and Society.* London: Vintage.

Freud, A. (1935). *Psychoanalysis for Teachers and Parents: Introductory Lectures.* New York: Emerson Books.

Newstead, S. (2005). *The Busker's Guide to Behaviour.* Eastleigh: Common Threads Publications.

Winnicott, D. W. (1969). *The Child, the Family and the Outside World.* Harmondsworth: Penguin.

Winnicott, D. W. (1971). *Playing and Reality.* London: Routledge.

Winnicott, D. W. (1984). *Deprivation and Delinquency.* London: Tavistock/Routledge.

Wiseman, R. (2002). *Queen Bees and Wannabees: Helping Your Daughter Survive Cliques, Gossip, Boyfriends and Other Realities of Adolescence.* London: Piatkus.

REFERENCES

Ainsworth, N. D. S. and Wittig, B. A. (1969). Attachment and Exploratory Behaviour of One-year-olds in a Strange Situation. In B. W. Foss (ed.), *Determination of Behaviour* (Vol. IV). London: Methuen, pp. 111–136.

Biddulph, S. (1997). *Raising Boys.* Sydney: Finch Publishing.

Bowlby, J. (1979). *The Making and Breaking of Affectional Bonds.* London: Tavistock Publications.

Chittenden, M. (2007). Mothers Boycott Pole-Dancing Toy. *The Sunday Times,* 4th March.

Clifford-Poston, A. (2005). *Tweens: What to Expect From, and How to Survive, Your Child's Pre-Teenage Years.* Oxford: Oneworld.

Clifford-Poston, A. (2007). *When Harry Hit Sally: Understanding Your Child's Behaviour.* London: Simon & Schuster.

Coren, A. (1997). *A Psychodynamic Approach to Education.* London: Sheldon Press.

Driscoll, M. (2003). Stealthily Stealing Their Innocence. *The Sunday Times,* 19th January.

Erikson, E. (1995). *Childhood and Society.* London: Vintage.

Freud, A. (1935). *Psychoanalysis for Teachers and Parents: Introductory Lectures.* New York: Emerson Books.

Freud, S. (1994). *Jokes and Their Relation to the Unconscious.* London: Penguin Books.

Gill, T. (2006). How to Improve the Nostalgic Parent. *Nursery World* (Out-of-School supplement), *106* (4015): 3, 13th April.

Guardian (2004). Five-year-olds Suffer Test Stress, 23rd August.

Hill, A. J. (2002). Developmental Issues in Attitudes to Food and Diet. *Proceedings of the Nutrition Society, 61*: 259–266.

Hobson, R. (1974). Loneliness. *The Journal of Analytic Psychology, 19* (1): 71–89.

Jackson, D. (2003). What's Got into the Tweenies? *The Times,* London, 28th July.

Klein, M. (1957). *Envy and Gratitude.* London: Tavistock Publications.

References

Klein, M. and Riviere, J. (1937). *Love, Hate and Reparation.* London: Hogarth.

Leach, P. (1997). *Your Baby and Child.* London: Penguin Books.

Lusseyran, J. J. (1999). *What One Sees Without Eyes: Selected Writings of Jacques Lusseyran.* Edinburgh: Floris Books.

Luxmoore, N. (2000). *Listening to Young People in School, Youth Work and Counselling.* London: Jessica Kingsley.

Maher, M. (1994). Bullying—The Lover, the Pimp and the Coward. *Educational Therapy and Therapeutic Teaching, 3:* 45–49.

Perez-Sanchez, M. (1990). *Baby Observation: Emotional Relationships During the First Year of Life.* Strathtay: Clunie Press.

Phillips, A. (1993). *On Kissing, Tickling and Being Bored.* London: Faber & Faber.

Phillips, A. (1996). *Terrors and Experts.* London: Faber & Faber.

Phillips, A. (1998). *The Beast in the Nursery.* London: Faber & Faber.

Royal College of Psychiatrists (2004). *Divorce or Separation of Parents—The Impact on Children and Adolescents: For Parents and Teachers,* RCP Fact Sheet 14.

Swinford, S. (2006). The School Bully is Moving into Cyberspace. *The Sunday Times,* 4th June.

Trenenan, A. (2002). Sugar, Spice and All Things Nasty. *The Times,* 6th August.

Winnicott, D. W. (1959). *The Family and Individual Development.* London: Tavistock; New York: Basic Books.

Winnicott, D. W. (1965). *The Maturational Processes and the Facilitating Environment.* London: Hogarth Press.

Winnicott, D. W. (1969). *The Child, the Family and the Outside World.* Harmondsworth: Penguin.

Winnicott, D. W. (1971). *Playing and Reality.* London: Routledge.

Winnicott, D. W. (1984). *Deprivation and Delinquency.* London: Tavistock/Routledge.

Wiseman, R. (2002). *Queen Bees and Wannabees: Helping Your Daughter Survive Cliques, Gossip, Boyfriends and Other Realities of Adolescence.* London: Piatkus.

INDEX